Whatever Happened to the Golden Plates?

Updated and revised August 2023

LDS Nonfiction by Jonathan Neville
The Lost City of Zarahemla
Moroni's America
Brought to Light
Letter VII: Joseph Smith and Oliver Cowdery Explain the Hill Cumorah
The Editors: Joseph, Don Carlos and William Smith
Whatever Happened to the Golden Plates?
Because of this Theory
Mesomania
Moroni's America (pocket edition)
The 2020 "seeing clearly" trilogy
- *A Man that Can Translate: Joseph Smith and the Nephite Interpreters (2d edition)*
- *Infinite Goodness: Joseph Smith, Jonathan Edwards, and the Language of the Book of Mormon*
- *Between these Hills: A Case for the New York Cumorah*

By Means of the Urim and Thummim: Restoring Translation to the Restoration (with James Lucas)

———

LDS fiction by Jonathan Neville

Before the World Finds Out
The Joy Helpers
Moroni's Keys
Among All Nations
In Earthly Things

———

Blogs
http://www.lettervii.com/
www.mobom.org
www.nomorecontention.com

Whatever Happened to the Golden Plates?

Updated and revised August 2023

Jonathan Neville, MS, JD

Whatever Happened to the Golden Plates?
Copyright © 2016, 2022, 2023 by Jonathan Neville
All rights reserved.
First Edition, Fifth Printing
8/26/23
This is a work of nonfiction. The author has made every effort to be accurate and complete and welcomes comments, suggestions, and corrections, which can be emailed to **lostzarahemla@gmail.com**.

All opinions expressed in this work are the responsibility of the author alone.

ISBN-13: 978-1544822723

ISBN-10: 1544822723

Front cover: Photograph taken by the author on the Hill Cumorah, New York.

Toll Free 1-877-222-1960

www.digitalegend.com

To open-minded people everywhere.

This book is dedicated to the Joseph Smith Papers and all those who created and have preserved historical records.

"He [Moroni] said this history was *written and deposited* not far from that place [Joseph Smith's home] …"
                                    Oliver Cowdery, Letter IV

NOTE TO READERS:

First, thanks for reading.
Nowadays, attention spans are short.
As is time.
We're all busy, and everyone wants our attention, so I'm humbled that you've given me yours.
I think the material in this book is important or I wouldn't have written it. So far as I know, what you're about to read is unique to this book.
(Otherwise I wouldn't have written it.)
It will be worth your time.

Second, thanks for your interest in LDS Church history. As more details emerge, the history of the Church becomes more and more faith-affirming.
This was supposed to be a small book, but the references accumulated and I couldn't figure out how to make it any shorter than it is.
If you're one of the readers who want more material, the Appendices are for you. To save printing costs, I've made even more information available online as indicated in the Appendices.

Whatever Happened to the Golden Plates?

Table of Contents

Selected Quotations – Cowdery, Ivins, Pratt viix
Timeline Summary xiii
Introduction – Why I Wrote this Book 1
Chapter 1 – The Saga of the Golden Plates 3
Chapter 2 – How Do We Know the Past? 8
Chapter 3 – What's New in Church History 12
Chapter 4 – Traditional Account 15
Chapter 5 – The 1829 Trip to Fayette 22
Chapter 6 – The Discovery of the Plates 39
Chapter 7 – What We Know about the Plates 49
Chapter 8 – Sealed plates 59
Chapter 9 – The Translation of the Plates 63
Chapter 9a – The order of translation. 64
Chapter 9b – The use of the plates 90
Chapter 10 – The Witnesses 107
Chapter 11 – Mormon "put them with" 117
Chapter 12 – Mormon's Repository 133
Chapter 13 – Handing them over 141
Chapter 14 – Whatever Happened to the Golden Plates?145
Appendix 1: Joseph Smith Papers 151
Appendix 2: Accounts of the 1829 Trip to Fayette 153
Appendix 3: The Lost 116 Pages 156
Appendix 4: Mormon and the Small Plates 156
Appendix 5: References on the Translation of the Book of
    Mormon 158
Appendix 6: The Sequence of the Translation of the Book of
    Mormon 160
Appendix 7: Accounts of the Trip to Fayette 162
Appendix 8: Philosophical Implications 162
Appendix 9: Two-Cumorahs background 165

Table of Figures

Figure 1 - Area Maps xii
Figure 2 - Customary route Harmony to Palmyra 31
Figure 3 - Alternative route Harmony to Palmyra 31
Figure 4 - Diagram of Two Sets of Plates 131
Figure 5 - Reenactment of translation table 169

Whatever Happened to the Golden Plates?

Selected Quotations

Oliver Cowdery wrote a series of 8 letters about Church history. They were originally published in the *Messenger and Advocate* in Kirtland in 1834 and 1835. Excerpts from Letter I are included in the Pearl of Great Price.

Letter III

"Since then our opposers have been thus kind to introduce our cause before the public, it is no more than just that a correct account should be given; and since they have invariably sought to cast a shade over the truth, and hinder its influence from gaining ascendancy, it is also proper that **it should be vindicated by laying before the world a correct statement of events as they have transpired from time to time.**

"Whether I shall succeed so far in my purpose as to convince the public of the incorrectness of those scurrilous reports which have inundated our land, or even but a small portion of them, will be better ascertained when I close than when I commence; **and I am content to submit it before the candid for perusal, and before the judge of all for inspection, as I most assuredly believe that before HIM I must stand and answer for the deeds transacted in this life.**

"Should I, however, be instrumental in causing **a few to hear before they judge, and understand both sides of this matter before they condemn,** I shall have the satisfaction of seeing them embrace it, as I am certain that one is the inevitable fruit of the other."

Letter IV

"He [Moroni] said this history was *written and deposited* not far from that place [Joseph's home]."

On April 6, 1928, President Anthony W. Ivins of the First Presidency spoke in General Conference about the Hill Cumorah in New York, which had recently been purchased by the Church.

"**Without doubt, these treasures lie concealed today, some of them, at least, to be brought forth in the not-distant future.** How soon this will be we do not know, but this is certain, we are more than a century nearer that time than we were at the time when Joseph Smith took from their resting place, in the hill Cumorah, the plates from which he translated the contents of the Book of Mormon.

"**All of these incidents to which I have referred, my brethren and sisters, are very closely associated with this particular spot in the state of New York.** Therefore I feel, as I said in the beginning of my remarks, that the acquisition of that spot of ground is more than an incident in the history of the Church; it is an epoch—an epoch which in my opinion is fraught with **that which may become of greater interest to the Latter-day Saints than that which has already occurred. We know that all of these records, all the sacred records of the Nephite people, were deposited by Mormon in that hill. That incident alone is sufficient to make it the sacred and hallowed spot that it is to us.**"

[See http://www.lettervii.com/2017/01/the-hill-cumorah-by-president-anthony-w.html]

Orson Pratt, an original member of the Quorum of the Twelve, wrote about Cumorah in the *Millennial Star* on July 7, 1866:

"**All the ancient plates, Mormon deposited in Cumorah,** about three hundred and eighty-four years after Christ. When Moroni, about thirty-six years after, made the deposit of the book entrusted to him, **he was, without doubt, inspired to select a department of the hill separate from the great sacred depository of the numerous volumes hid up by his father.**

"The particular place in the hill, where Moroni secreted the book, was revealed, by the angel, to the Prophet Joseph Smith, to whom the volume was delivered in September, A.D. 1827. **But the grand repository of all the numerous records of the ancient nations of the western continent, was located in another department of the hill…**

"The hill Cumorah, with the surrounding vicinity, is distinguished as the great battle-field on which, and near which, two powerful nations were concentrated with all their forces, men, women, and children, and fought till hundreds of thousands on both sides were hewn down, and left to moulder upon the ground…"

[See http://www.lettervii.com/2016/08/the-hill-cumorah-sacred-depository.html]

Figure 1 - Area Maps (adapted from maps on churchofjesuschrist.org)

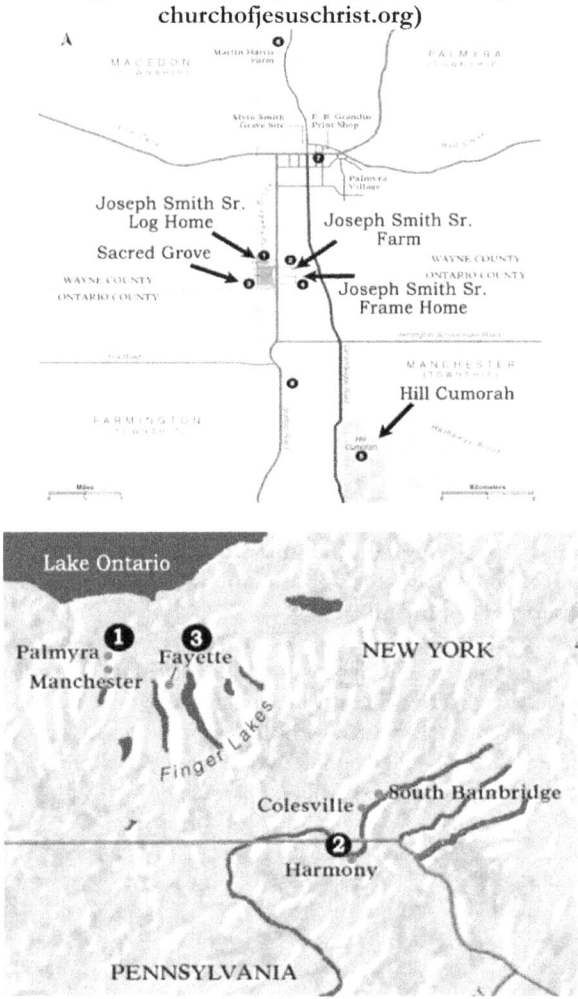

Whatever Happened to the Golden Plates?

Timeline Summary

September 1823. Moroni visits Joseph. Joseph visits the Hill Cumorah and sees the plates for the first time.

September 1827. Joseph obtains the plates from Cumorah.

December 1827. Joseph and Emma move to Harmony, PA.

April-June 1828. Martin Harris writes as Joseph translates the first part of the plates (the Book of Lehi on 116 pages).

July 1828. Joseph learns Martin Harris lost the 116 pages.

April-May 1829. At Harmony, PA, Oliver writes as Joseph continues the translation of the original plates he obtained from Moroni, as described on the Title Page: Mormon's abridgment of the record of the Nephites, Moroni's abridgment of the record of Ether, and Moroni's concluding comments. This is Mosiah through Moroni in the current Book of Mormon. In April, the Lord promises Oliver that when he and Joseph finish the record they have in Harmony, there are other records that Oliver will have power to assist to translate (D&C 9:1-2)

May 1829. When Joseph and Oliver near the completion of the Harmony translation, they consider starting over at the beginning. The Lord tells them not to retranslate the Book of Lehi (the 116 pages lost by Martin Harris). Instead, they must translate the unabridged plates of Nephi directly (D&C 10:38-51). But they don't yet have the small plates.

May 1829. Through the Urim and Thummim, Joseph receives a revelation to ask David Whitmer to come to Harmony immediately to transport Joseph and Oliver to the home of Peter Whitmer (David's father) near Fayette. Oliver writes the letter.

May 1829. Before leaving Harmony, Joseph and Oliver translate the Title Page from the last leaf of the original plates. They have this page printed to submit as part of a copyright application, which is filed on June 11 at Utica, NY.

May 1829. Before leaving Harmony, Joseph gives the plates to a divine messenger with a promise that when he gets to Fayette, he will receive the plates he needs to translate there.

May 1829. David Whitmer receives Oliver's letter but can't leave because of farm work. Miraculously, three unknown persons plow his fields and spread plaster (fertilizer) so he can go.

May-June 1829. Joseph monitors David's progress using the Urim and Thummim and relates the details to Oliver, who records them. David verifies every detail on the return trip.

June 1829. On their way from Harmony to Fayette, New York, Joseph, Oliver, and David meet a divine messenger who is carrying the plates and says he is going to Cumorah, a place David had never heard of previously.

June 1829. In Fayette, Joseph receives the plates of Nephi from a divine messenger (who presumably brought them from the Cumorah repository). He translates the small plates of Nephi (1 Nephi - Words of Mormon).

June 1829. Joseph, Oliver, David and Martin Harris see the plates as shown to them by an angel.

June or July 1829. The Eight Witnesses see and handle the plates as shown to them by Joseph Smith.

1829-1830. On multiple occasions, Joseph, Oliver and others visit the room in Cumorah that contains Mormon's repository of Nephite records and artifacts (Mormon 6:6). They apparently move the records from Cumorah to a nearby location.

A complete chronology is available online here: http://www.josephsmithpapers.org/reference/events

The Sept. 2015 *Ensign* has an excellent overview of the events in Harmony, Pennsylvania, online at this link:

https://www.churchofjesuschrist.org/study/ensign/2015/09/joseph-smith-in-harmony?lang=eng

Introduction – Why I Wrote this Book

I wrote this book to share what I consider an exciting new development in Church history. It has always been assumed that Joseph Smith translated one set of plates—the ones he got from the box in the Hill Cumorah. But my research suggests that there were in fact *two separate sets*.

Joseph obtained the first set of plates from Moroni's stone box on the Hill Cumorah in New York in 1827. This set contained abridgments by Mormon and Moroni as described on the Title Page. Joseph translated these plates in Harmony, Pennsylvania. He gave the plates to a divine messenger when he finished and then moved to Fayette.

The second set, commonly referred to as the "small plates of Nephi," was delivered to Joseph in Fayette, New York. He translated the second set as 1 Nephi through Words of Mormon.

If true, this insight may reconcile details of Church history that have seemed out of place, random, or just strange. Previously inexplicable accounts now fit together to answer important questions that continue to gnaw at us today. Questions such as:

"Where did Joseph get the plates of Nephi?"

[If you think they were part of the record Moroni left in the box on Cumorah, you will be surprised when you take another look at material you've read your entire life.]

"Where was the repository of Nephite records Mormon mentioned in Mormon 6:6?"

And, of course, "Whatever happened to the golden plates?"

———

The second reason why I wrote this book is to expand on the second chapter of my short book titled *Letter VII: Oliver Cowdery's Message to the World about the Hill Cumorah* (2nd Edition). There, I discussed the question of the "Mesoamerican/two-

Cumorahs" theory (M2C). This theory claims that the Book of Mormon took place in Central America (primarily in Mesoamerica, meaning southern Mexico and Guatemala—the home of the Mayans).[1]

According to this theory, New York is too far away from Mesoamerica to be the scene of the final battles of the Nephites and Jaredites. This leads to the conclusion that Joseph and Oliver were speculating when they said these final battles took place in New York—and they were wrong.

I disagree with the two-Cumorahs theory for reasons I've explained in *Moroni's America* and other books. The evidence presented in this book challenges the two-Cumorahs theory from a purely historical perspective.

If you haven't read Chapter 2 of my *Letter VII* book, I have provided a short explanation in Appendix 9.

For a broader discussion of the plates, I highly recommend Richard Bushman's book, *Joseph Smith's Gold Plates: a cultural history*, published by Oxford University Press in 2023. Appendix B, "The Translation Debates," includes a discussion of the "two-sets of plates" scenario described in this book, as well as various theories about the translation process.

---

[1] I address this in *The Lost City of Zarahemla*.

1 The Saga of the Golden Plates

My basic thesis could fit in a tweet: "Joseph translated two separate sets of plates."

This concept is so obvious to me now that it's difficult to remember thinking he translated only one set.

And yet, the one-set interpretation of Church history has been taken for granted for decades. Maybe it's never been challenged before.

Arthur Schopenhauer's observation is overused, but I think it applies here because my simple tweet, by itself, is not going to overcome the long-held assumption.

> All truth passes through three stages.
> First, it is ridiculed.
> Second, it is violently opposed.
> Third, it is accepted as being self-evident.

The rest of this book explains the rationale for my thesis. It's possible that for some people, the idea alone will suffice. They'll think back on what they know of Church history and realize that the two-sets-of-plates theory explains a lot of things. It makes sense of the Title Page and D&C 9 and 10. If you already get it, you're done.

Quickest read ever.

But if you're like me, you want to explore the facts and the reasoning. So here goes.

The saga of the golden plates is one of the first things anyone learns about Mormonism. It remains a focus for both believers and critics because the veracity of everything else Joseph and his contemporaries claimed depends largely on whether the ancient plates really existed.

And yet, after nearly two centuries, perplexing questions of history remain unresolved.

The basics can be easily summarized. Believers accept Joseph Smith, Jr.'s explanation that, as directed by an angel named Moroni in 1823, he found ancient metal plates in a stone box on a hill in western New York. Moroni, an ancient prophet who lived in America, had deposited the plates in that location around 421 A.D. The plates were engraved in an unknown language. By the gift and power of God, Joseph translated the record into English, dictating the text to scribes. When the translation was complete, eleven men were allowed to see the plates for themselves before Joseph returned them to the care of the angel. Joseph published the record as the Book of Mormon. The plates have not been seen since.

As you know (or can imagine) each of the sentences in the preceding paragraph is pregnant with controversy. Critics accept only the last two, claiming Joseph made up the rest and thereby perpetrated a fraud.

The details of the saga are the topic of innumerable articles, books, and blogs because the historical record lends itself to multiple interpretations.

For example, the Three Witnesses and the Eight Witnesses provided formal, signed declarations about their respective experiences. But from the outset, critics noticed that the witnesses gave different descriptions of the plates.

The hearsay nature of historical accounts—people reporting on what others have said—naturally gives rise to discrepancies. But the witnesses themselves did, in fact, give a range of descriptions. If the witnesses all saw and handled the same plates, how could their descriptions differ?

Beyond describing the plates themselves, the witnesses gave varying accounts of the circumstances in which they saw the plates. They also spoke of other events involving the plates that faithful historians tend to bypass because they don't fit the generally accepted narrative.

Whatever Happened to the Golden Plates?

Aside from the historical problems, the saga of the plates raises questions of scriptural interpretation.

For example, the Title Page of the Book of Mormon, taken, as Joseph said, "from the **very last leaf, on the left hand side of the collection or book of plates,**" describes two sets of abridgments but no original plates. Yet the original, unabridged small plates of Nephi make up about 26% of the text we have today. Why was this important material omitted from the Title Page?

Joseph also said the English Title Page "is a genuine and literal translation of the Title Page of the ***Original* Book of Mormon**, as recorded on the plates." [Emphasis added.] We normally think the term "original" refers to the plates, but that makes the last clause redundant. It's true we don't currently have the "original" Book of Mormon because Martin Harris lost the first 116 pages that were translated, but could Joseph be telling us something more here?

The Title Page, combined with Joseph's explanation, suggests that the "original" Book of Mormon—the one on the set of plates Moroni deposited in the stone box—*did not contain the small plates of Nephi*. Instead, Joseph had to obtain those plates separately. As we will see later in this book, D&C 9 and 10 may have told us this all along.

Critics, of course, pounce on the perplexities to cast doubt on everything. In my view, the explanation that Joseph translated two separate sets of plates offers a useful response to critics and gives us greater insight into the miraculous and profound saga of the golden plates.

A General Conference was held in Ohio on 25-26 October, 1831. All 11 witnesses of the plates attended.[2] The minutes of the meeting relate that

> Br. Hyrum Smith said that he thought best that the information of the coming forth of the book of Mormon be related by Joseph himself to the Elders present that all might know for themselves. Br. Joseph Smith jr. said that it was not intended to tell the world all the particulars of the coming forth of the book of Mormon, & also said that it was not expedient for him to relate these things &c."[3]

Scholars have interpreted this to refer to the *translation*, but that's not the term Hyrum and Joseph said.

The minutes here are incomplete, as we can see from the "&c." at the end of the sentence. When considered in context and in light of subsequent events, the incomplete minutes of Joseph's 1831 statement likely meant that it was not expedient *at that meeting* for Joseph to relate these things.

No reasonable historian can argue that the 1831 statement precluded subsequent statements about the "coming forth of the Book of Mormon," particularly because Joseph himself *did* provide more details in the later statements—as did other participants in the 1831 meeting, including Oliver Cowdery, John Whitmer, Orson Pratt, Martin Harris, and David Whitmer.

This meeting took place in 1831. Joseph didn't produce his first known account of the coming forth of the Book of Mormon until 1832.

The first detailed account was not published until 1834-5 (Oliver Cowdery's eight historical essays, with which Joseph assisted). The *Elders' Journal* account of the translation was

---

[2] See *Minutes*, 25-26 October 1831, Historical Introduction, online at http://www.josephsmithpapers.org/paper-summary/minutes-25-26-october-1831/1#historical-intro.

[3] *Minutes*, 25-26 October 1831, available online at http://www.josephsmithpapers.org/paper-summary/minutes-25-26-october-1831/4.

published in 1838. Joseph's own detailed account was not compiled until 1838 and wasn't published until 1842. The Wentworth letter was also published in 1842, and the "Latter Day Saints" article was published in 1844.

Each of these post-1831 statements about the "coming forth of the Book of Mormon" added particulars to the historical record, but gaps in the record remain.

The phrase "coming forth of the Book of Mormon" encompasses more than just the translation. Some of the people present actually did subsequently give particulars of what they thought they observed regarding the *translation*, but none of them gave the particulars of the specific aspects of the "coming forth" that I address in this book.

The gradual release of information about the "coming forth of the Book of Mormon" makes sense because circumstances changed. The growth and expansion of the Church meant that fewer people could have personal interactions with Joseph Smith. He and Oliver needed to document their experiences for future generations as well.

We can see from the 1834 *Mormonism Unvailed* that various accounts of the translation were circulating. That book pointed out that the idea of a "translation" produced by reading words of the stone in the hat (SITH) without reference to the plates not only undermined the credibility of the narrative Joseph provided, but also made the testimony of the witnesses about those plates irrelevant.

Ultimately, the historical record establishes that Joseph and Oliver wanted people to know that Joseph Smith translated the engravings on the plates by means of the Urim and Thummim that came with the plates; i.e., that God had prepared the special instrument that Joseph used to translate the ancient record. This meant that there was no possibility of a source for the text that was not divine.

2 How Do We Know the Past?

The title of this book explains its main focus. We all want to know what happened to the golden plates.

Maybe someday Moroni will give us more details—after all, he holds the keys of the Book of Mormon (D&C 27:5)—but for now, we can learn quite a bit from taking another look at the historical material we already have.

Because I am not a professional historian, I need to explain my approach to studying history.

Historical events are set in stone—we can't change the past. But our *understanding* of those events is fluid. To see why, let's consider this question:

How do we know the history of the Church?

We are fortunate to have lots of records, including journals, documents, correspondence, newspaper reports, and official histories. But none of these tells a complete story unless put in context, which introduces subjectivity.

In a sense, trial lawyers are historians. They seek to understand past events and make them understandable to a fact-finding authority (judge or jury) in a manner favorable to their clients. Litigation is usually a debate about history.

When I practiced law, I had stints as both a criminal prosecutor and a criminal defense lawyer. My opponents and I would examine every known bit of evidence to assemble a coherent and consistent account of what happened in the past. Often, the facts were so indisputable that a guilty verdict was a foregone conclusion, and a guilty plea resulted. But other times, extensive research leads the two sides to completely different versions of history, and the only way to resolve the dispute is at trial.

That's what I see happening with some details in Church history. The evidence is ambiguous or even contradictory, and we end up with multiple theories about what happened and why.

Whatever Happened to the Golden Plates?

"The dog that didn't bark" was a famously obscure clue that led Sherlock Holmes to solve a mystery.

My work in Church history has focused on similar clues. When I investigated the authorship of the anonymous articles in the *Times and Seasons*, the dog that didn't bark was a list of books donated to the Nauvoo Library in 1844 (see *The Lost City of Zarahemla*). When I investigated Book of Mormon passages about geography, the dog that didn't bark was a reference to "west sea south" (Alma 53:8) (see *Moroni's America*).

The dog that didn't bark in this book was an unusual comment by David Whitmer about encountering an old man bearing a knapsack. In June 1829, David was driving his wagon from Harmony to Fayette with Joseph and Oliver as passengers. He stopped to give the man a ride, but the man declined, explaining he was going to Cumorah.

That comment nagged at me. The few historians who even mentioned the event dismissed it as a product of David's faulty memory, probably conflated with a false tradition about Cumorah.

But that didn't make sense to me. I pulled on the thread, and the result is this book.

History begins every second; you can't go back in time even to the moment you read the previous sentence. The persistence of memory makes life seem fluid, similar to the way persistence of vision makes a movie seem continuous. Movies consist of a series of still images displayed at the rate of 24 frames per second. We don't perceive each discreet image separately because our mind interpolates between each image. We make a connection. We smooth it out.

Likewise, we process events as discreet moments. We usually don't notice the details of an event unless we relate it or write it down—or unless we're asked about it. Then we draw on our memories to see what our brains may have recorded about the event.

Defects in perception and recall make even eyewitness testimony problematic. On a daily basis, courts around the world confront discrepancies between the testimony of multiple people whose eyes may have witnessed the same event, but whose brains recorded it differently. *Much* differently in many cases.

Often a particular historical narrative takes on the qualities of "truth" because it is widely accepted, but all understanding of history is inherently subjective. We have no photographs from the 1830s. No video or audio recordings. All we have are personal accounts, historical documents, and limited physical evidence.

Records kept by eyewitness accounts are usually the only sources for historical information, but no two people can observe the same event in identical ways. Each person has a unique perceptual filter, based on past experience, expectations, and priorities. Memories are imperfect and fade over time. Relatively few people keep journals, and even the most meticulous and detailed journals are inherently incomplete.

Understanding history is a subjective endeavor.

We examine historical records in the totality of the circumstances, considering not only the words on a page but the personalities and motivations of the authors and the circumstances in which they lived. Sometimes a new historical document surfaces that completely changes our understanding of past events. Other times a fresh look brings an entirely new interpretation of existing documents.

Church historians and private collectors have done a remarkable job acquiring, assembling, and organizing most of the sources I use in this book. Many are relatively obscure and unknown to most readers, but whether or not you have read them before doesn't matter.

We're going to take that fresh look.

I think of historical references as keys on a piano. Each key strikes the same wire no matter who presses it, but together they can be played in unlimited variations.

Whatever Happened to the Golden Plates?

Like piano keys, the words in historical sources are fixed. But as we interpret them through our own filters of unique experiences, priorities, interests, and insights into human nature, we can derive multiple interpretations.

Ideally, the more perspectives we consider, the closer we'll come to the truth. But whether we actually reach the truth is for the factfinder—you, in this case—to decide.

3 What's New in Church History

When we study history, we're studying the past. Nothing "new" can happen in the past.

What's done is done.

But what we *know* about the past can, and often does, change.

In the last decade or so, there have been many discoveries in Church history. When historical documents are uncovered or found (or disclosed) for the first time, they are new to us. When organized and placed in context, new documents lead to new insights and connections.

The Joseph Smith Papers project continues to provide new documents and better, more accessible organization so historians and people such as you and me can make new connections and develop new insights into events we may have known, at least in general terms, our entire lives.

This book proposes some connections that may appear new to you, including these:
- Joseph and Oliver translated two separate sets of plates
- The plates Joseph translated are still in New York
- They are with the Nephite repository
- The repository is not far from the Hill Cumorah

Among other things these connections mean there is only one Cumorah and it is in New York. I hope that is obvious to you. If not, review Appendix 9.

If you're familiar with LDS history and doctrine, you know that Joseph Smith made some extraordinary claims about experiences he had starting in the 1820s.

Here's a quick review.

Joseph was born on December 23, 1805, making him a teenager when these life-changing events began.

Whatever Happened to the Golden Plates?

First, in 1820 God and the resurrected Jesus Christ appeared to Joseph and told him not to join any of the Churches in his area (upstate New York, specifically Palmyra, a small town on the Erie Canal about twenty miles southeast from Rochester.)

Second, in 1823 an ancient American prophet named Moroni, having been resurrected, appeared to Joseph and told him that a record of his ancient people had been written and deposited not far from his home. Moroni, who had buried the metal plates around 421 A.D., told Joseph to retrieve the record and translate it. Joseph spent four years in preparation, visiting the site annually on the autumn equinox, before finally taking possession.

Third, Joseph translated the ancient record, using special interpreters left by Moroni with the plates which he called the Urim and Thummim. He dictated the entire Book of Mormon (named after Moroni's father, who abridged most of the account) to various scribes, principally Oliver Cowdery.

Neither Joseph nor Oliver described the translation process in detail. Although others claimed to have observed the work, their accounts are inconsistent in some details. Other third-hand accounts generate more heat than light.

Fourth, three witnesses—Oliver Cowdery, David Whitmer, and Martin Harris—testified that an angel appeared to them and showed them the plates.

Fifth, eight witnesses testified that Joseph Smith showed them the plates, which they handled.

Sixth, the current whereabouts of the plates is unknown. Joseph returned the plates to the angel, who said he would call for them (Joseph Smith-History 1:59), but Joseph gave no details about when and where this occurred. Others did provide details, which are discussed in this book.

If it seems strange to you that we have so few details about the plates, I agree. Because the Book of Mormon is the keystone of our religion, and these events took place less than 200 years ago, one would think we should have a more coherent understanding of what happened when, to whom, and how.

But maybe we actually know more than we realize.

The evidence has been here all along, but we didn't see how it all fit. Many accounts of events in Church history have seemed out-of-place or random, if not inexplicable.

When viewed through the two-sets-of-plates theory, they make sense. They fit a coherent, faith-sustaining narrative.

You might ask, why have these accounts remained outside the traditional narrative, like puzzle pieces on the floor that few people noticed? Or maybe they've been on the table, face up, but we couldn't see how they fit?

Clearly, these pieces don't fit the puzzle defined by the two-Cumorahs theory.

For example, Brigham Young spoke of a room in the Hill Cumorah that was full of Nephite records and other artifacts. This would be the place Mormon described in Mormon 6:6.

Brigham said Oliver and Joseph visited the room at least twice. But if the records repository is in New York, it can't be in Central America, and the two-Cumorahs theory is false.

That's not easy for some people to accept.

Consequently, the two-Cumorahs theory holds that Brigham's account involved a spiritual vision, not an actual visit. Later in this book we'll look at all the accounts of the records repository, but for now, you can see why people are confused about such events in Church history.

In this book, we want to help eliminate the confusion and to reconcile the various accounts into an accurate, factually supported narrative. These accounts are missing pieces that now complete the puzzle.

Certainly my proposals are subject to your own analysis. You might reach different conclusions. If so, I hope you share them. Working together, eventually we'll get the history right.

Or as close to what really happened as possible.

4 Traditional Account

For Latter-day Saints, the most familiar source of Church history is Joseph Smith-History, the 6,400-word account canonized in the Pearl of Great Price in 1880. The 75 verses in this account begin with Joseph's birth and continue through the 1829 baptisms of Joseph and Oliver Cowdery. Joseph and his contemporaries began composing this history in 1838, relying on unrecorded memories to supplement the few historical documents that existed. This history was serialized in the *Times and Seasons* between March 15, 1842 and August 1, 1842.

Joseph Smith-History is part of the larger history designated by the Joseph Smith Papers as "History, circa June 1839-circa 1841 [Draft 2]."[4] Joseph and his scribes worked on the history but did not complete it before his death in 1844. Draft 2 was used with other sources to compile the well-known *History of the Church*, which has been cited in official lesson manuals and in works by Church authorities as well as scholars, educators, and members generally.

The *History of the Church* was a serviceable compilation, but it included considerable editorial interpretation. For example, several third-person sources were converted to the first person as though Joseph Smith composed them.

Much better references are available through the Joseph Smith Papers. See Appendix I for more detail.

There are other sources of Church history, including Church-affiliated newspapers and other publications, private journals and correspondence not included in the Joseph Smith Papers, and observations made by outsiders, including both published and unpublished sources.

---

[4] The original document and useful historical information may be found at http://www.josephsmithpapers.org/paper-summary/history-circa-june-1839-circa-1841-draft-2/1.

New material is being added whenever it is discovered.

We have never had as many historical sources available as we do now. We have original documents that earlier historians didn't have.

And yet, our understanding of history remains a subjective interpretation of the evidence, usually guided by long-held traditions. This is to be expected. Church historians are educated and trained by previous Church historians, so interpretations tend to taken for granted and passed along. There's no reason to reinvent the wheel with each generation.

But Groupthink can be problematic if we are not cognizant of it. It's healthy to step away from our preconceptions to take a new look at the evidence.

The traditional account of aspects of early Church history is summarized in the book, *Our Heritage*[5], on churchofjesuschrist.org. The excerpts below cover the translation of the Book of Mormon and the experiences of the Three Witnesses which I will discuss in more detail throughout this book.

Notice the citations in the excerpt. They include the *History of the Church*, Lucy Mack Smith's account which she dictated in 1845 after Joseph's death, and early journals and recollections.

Nothing about this history is incorrect; after all, it's merely a brief overview. Presumably you are familiar with the narrative, but it's important for you to read it again so you have a context for the later chapters in this book.

I've put important passages in **bold**. The footnotes in this section are from the original book.

---

[5] The book is available online at
https://www.churchofjesuschrist.org/manual/our-heritage/title-page?lang=eng

Whatever Happened to the Golden Plates?

The Work of Translation

On 22 September 1827, after four years of preparation, Moroni gave the Prophet Joseph the gold plates and told him to begin the work of translation. **Emma Hale**, whom Joseph had married earlier that year, **accompanied him on that occasion and was waiting at the foot of the Hill Cumorah when her husband returned with the plates**. She became an important help to the Prophet and **acted as one of the Book of Mormon scribes for a brief period**.

Because of the repeated and strenuous efforts of a local mob to steal the gold plates, Joseph and Emma were forced to leave their home in Manchester, New York. They took refuge at the home of Emma's father, Isaac Hale, in Harmony, Pennsylvania, about 120 miles southeast of Manchester. There Joseph began translating the plates. He was soon joined by his friend, Martin Harris, a well-to-do farmer, who became his scribe.

Martin asked Joseph if he could take 116 pages of translated material home to show his family members to prove to them the validity of the work they were doing. Joseph asked the Lord for permission, but the Lord's answer was no. Martin pleaded for Joseph to ask again, which Joseph reluctantly did two more times and finally received permission. Martin made a covenant to show the manuscript only to certain people, but he broke his promise, and **the pages of manuscript were stolen**. This loss caused Joseph inconsolable grief, for he thought that all his efforts to serve the Lord had been lost. He cried, "What shall I do? I have sinned—it is I who tempted the wrath of God. I should have been satisfied with the first answer which I received from the Lord."[6]

Joseph sincerely repented, and **after a brief period when the plates and the Urim and Thummim were taken away,** the Lord forgave him and he began translating once again. **The Lord instructed him not to retranslate the lost material, which**

---

[6] Lucy Mack Smith, *History of Joseph Smith* (1958), 128.

contained a secular history. Instead, Joseph was to translate other plates prepared by the prophet Nephi that covered the same period of time but contained greater prophecies of Christ and other sacred writings. **The Lord had foreseen the loss of the 116 pages and inspired Nephi to prepare this second history.** (See 1 Nephi 9; D&C 10:38–45; see also D&C 3 and D&C 10, which were received during this period.)

At this time, Joseph was blessed with the help of Oliver Cowdery, a young schoolteacher who was directed by the Lord to the Prophet's home. Oliver commenced to write on 7 April 1829. Of that momentous time he said, "These were days never to be forgotten—to sit under the sound of a voice dictated by the inspiration of heaven, awakened the utmost gratitude of this bosom!" **(JS—H 1:71, footnote)**.

Oliver further declared: "That book is true. ... **I wrote it myself as it fell from the lips of the Prophet.** It contains the everlasting gospel, and comes in fulfillment of the revelations of John where it says he saw an angel come with the everlasting gospel to preach to every nation, tongue and people. It contains principles of salvation. And if you will walk by its light and obey its precepts you will be saved in the everlasting kingdom of God."[7]

In the midst of their work, Joseph and Oliver found that their dedication to the translation of the record had left them without food or money; they lacked even the necessary writing materials. Learning of their plight, Joseph Knight Sr., a former employer and friend of the Prophet, determined to give them assistance. He described the nature of his most timely aid:

"I bought a barrel of mackerel and some lined paper for writing. ... I bought some nine or ten bushels of grain and five or six bushels taters [potatoes]." He then visited the two men in Harmony and recalled that "Joseph and Oliver were gone to see

---

[7] *Reuben Miller Journals*, 1848–49, 21 Oct. 1848; Historical Department, Archives Division, The Church of Jesus Christ of Latter-day Saints; hereafter cited as LDS Church Archives; spelling and punctuation modernized.

if they could find a place to work for provisions, but found none. They returned home and found me there with provisions, and they were glad for they were out. … **Then they went to work and had provisions enough to last till the translation was done."**[8]

Is it any wonder that the Prophet Joseph said of this righteous man: "It shall be said of him, by the sons of Zion, while there is one of them remaining, that this man was a faithful man in Israel; therefore his name shall never be forgotten."[9]

Because of increasing persecution, Joseph and Oliver left Harmony and completed the work of translation at the Peter Whitmer farm in Fayette, New York, during June 1829. The completion of this work in the midst of such trying circumstances is truly a modern-day miracle. With little formal education, Joseph Smith dictated the translation in just a little over two months of actual working time and made very few corrections. The book stands today essentially as he translated it and has been the source of testimony for millions of people throughout the world. Joseph Smith was a powerful instrument in the hands of the Lord in bringing forth the words of ancient prophets for the blessing of Saints in the latter days.

Witnesses to the Book of Mormon

While the Prophet Joseph Smith was in Fayette, the Lord revealed that Oliver Cowdery, David Whitmer, and Martin Harris were to be **three special witnesses who would be permitted to see the gold plates** (see 2 Nephi 27:12; Ether 5:2–4; D&C 17). They, along with Joseph, would be able to testify of the origin and truth of this ancient record.

David Whitmer explained: "We went out into the woods, near by, and sat down on a log and talked awhile. We then kneeled down and prayed. Joseph prayed. We then got up and sat on the log and

---

[8] Dean Jessee, ed., "Joseph Knight's Recollection of Early Mormon History," *BYU Studies*, Autumn 1976, 36; spelling modernized.
[9] *History of the Church*, 5:124–25.

were talking, when **all at once a light came down from above us and encircled us for quite a little distance around; and the angel stood before us.**" This angel was Moroni. David said that he "was dressed in white, and spoke and called me by name and said 'Blessed is he that keepeth His commandments.' A table was set before us and on it the records were placed. **The Records of the Nephites, from which the Book of Mormon was translated, the brass plates, the Ball of Directors, the sword of Laban and other plates.**"[10] While the men were viewing these things, they heard a voice that said: "These plates have been revealed by the power of God, and they have been translated by the power of God. The translation of them which you have seen is correct, and I command you to bear record of what you now see and hear."[11]

Soon after this event, Joseph Smith showed the plates to eight additional witnesses, who handled them in a secluded setting near the Smith family home in Manchester, New York. The testimonies of both groups of witnesses are recorded at the beginning of the Book of Mormon.

As you know (or can imagine), the momentous events summarized in the preceding section have prompted biographers, historians, theologians, and any number of other professionals and other authors to write innumerable articles and books.

More than most of us can hope to read.

I wouldn't have added to the pile unless I thought there was something missing from the traditional interpretations.

Right up front, in the Introduction and in Chapter 2, I summarized my proposals. The rest of this book will evaluate the evidence upon which I rely.

---

[10] *The Saints' Herald*, 1 Mar. 1882, 68.
[11] *History of the Church*, 1:55.

Whatever Happened to the Golden Plates?

But I want to point out an important detail. Did you notice the reference to **JS—H 1:71, footnote** in the extract on page 19 above? That note is an extract from Oliver Cowdery's "Letter I," the first in the series of his eight important letters about Church history.

"Letter VII" (Letter Seven) discusses the Hill Cumorah in detail. I wrote an entire book about it.[12]

---

[12] Jonathan Neville, *Letter VII: Oliver Cowdery's Message to the World about the Hill Cumorah*, 2nd Edition (2016).

5 The 1829 Trip to Fayette

A little-known incident in Church history, related on several occasions by David Whitmer,[13] plays a significant role in understanding what happened to the golden plates.

David said that when he took Joseph and Oliver from Harmony to Fayette in June 1829, he encountered an old man along the road who said he was going to Cumorah. David, who had lived in the area most of his life, had never heard of Cumorah. He asked Joseph about it. Joseph identified the man as a divine messenger who was carrying the plates.

The obvious question is, why would a divine messenger carry the plates to Cumorah if Joseph was going to continue translating them in Fayette?

That question prompted the inquiry that led to my conclusion that Joseph translated two sets of plates.

My conclusion relies on many elements that I'll discuss in later chapters. I think the best way for me to explain is to follow the steps I took during my investigation, starting with the 1829 trip to Fayette. Then we'll go back in time to the discovery of the plates, what we know about the plates, the order of translation, the use of the plates, and so forth until we reach the final question, whatever happened to the golden plates?

The "old man taking plates to Cumorah" incident doesn't fit the traditional narrative, so it is usually bypassed in books about Church history. Some authors question David Whitmer's reliability and credibility because of what he said. I think that's a mistake for reasons I'll address later in this chapter and in Appendix 2.

---

[13] See Appendix 7.

Those unfamiliar with the geography of this area should refer to this map.

Areas where Joseph, Oliver, and David lived and worked during 1828-1830.
From https://www.churchofjesuschrist.org/study/scriptures/history-maps/map-1?lang=eng.

The 1829 trip from Harmony to Fayette involved a series of divine interventions that underscore the importance of the event.

1. In May, when they were nearing the end of the translation, Joseph and Oliver considered returning to the beginning to retranslate the Book of Lehi (the 116 pages lost by Martin Harris). By revelation (D&C 10), the Lord told Joseph not to retranslate the Book of Lehi but instead to translate the plates of Nephi.

2. Joseph was told, through the Urim and Thummim, to contact David Whitmer, a man he had never met, and tell him

to come immediately to Harmony. David was to take Joseph and Oliver to his father's home in Fayette so they could finish translating the Book of Mormon.

3. May being prime planting season, David couldn't suddenly take a week off to travel to Harmony. However, unknown strangers plowed his fields overnight and spread fertilizer, enabling him to leave.

4. Joseph closely followed David's trip, telling Oliver where he stayed and whom he met. Oliver wrote this down in a notebook.

5. Before leaving Harmony, Joseph gave the plates to a divine messenger for safekeeping and transportation.

6. Before David arrived in Harmony, Joseph knew he was coming. He and Oliver began walking and met David along the route, saving time.

7. Oliver asked David about his journey and verified every detail Joseph had related. This confirmed Joseph's prophetic abilities for both men.

8. During the trip to Fayette, the group met the old man who was taking the plates to Cumorah.

9. After they arrived at the Whitmer home, Joseph obtained the plates and completed the translation.

10. A messenger showed the plates to David's mother to console her for the extra work she had to do boarding Joseph and Oliver.

One striking feature of these events is the sense of urgency. Joseph is commanded to tell David to come immediately, divine intervention makes that possible, and Joseph supernaturally monitors David's progress from Fayette to Harmony.

The other striking feature is the separate pathways of the people and the plates. David, Joseph and Oliver travel directly from Harmony to Fayette. The plates don't. They make a detour to Cumorah before showing up in Fayette.

Why?

Whatever Happened to the Golden Plates?

According to the traditional version of events, Moroni's stone box on Cumorah was empty. There was no reason for the divine messenger to take the plates there.

But the traditional version doesn't account for the repository of Nephite records and artifacts in the Hill Cumorah.

In Mormon 6:6, Mormon explained that he "hid up in the hill Cumorah all the records which had been entrusted to me by the hand of the Lord, save it were these few plates which I gave unto my son Moroni."

Brigham Young and others said this repository was in the Hill Cumorah in New York. Joseph, Oliver and others visited it multiple times.

If, as I propose, Joseph had completed the translation of the plates he received from Moroni, he had no further use for those plates. It made sense to give them to the messenger who would return them to the repository that was in the Hill Cumorah.

The Lord commanded Joseph to translate the plates of Nephi. Where would he get those?

From the repository.

The same messenger who took the original plates to the repository picked up the plates of Nephi and brought them to Fayette. Alternatively, another messenger may have brought the plates of Nephi to Fayette while the first messenger took the original plates to the repository.

Either way, Joseph translated two sets of plates.

If that summary is sufficient for you, skip to the next chapter. For the rest of this chapter, we're going to look at the actual accounts.

In May 1829, when Joseph and Oliver were nearing completion of the translation of the plates Joseph possessed in Harmony, they were commanded to move to the home of the Whitmer family near Fayette, New York.

Lucy Mack Smith explained how this came about. After describing a court case in Palmyra involving Martin and Lucy Harris, Lucy Mack wrote:

> In the meantime Joseph was 150 miles distant and knew naught of the matter e[x]cept an intimation that was given through the urim and thumim for as he one morning applied the<m> ~~latter~~ to his eyes to look upon the record instead of the words of the book being given him he was commanded to write a letter to one David Whitmore [Whitmer] this man Joseph had never seen but he was instructed to say him that he must come with his team immediately in order to convey Joseph and his family <Oliver [Cowdery]> back to his house which was 135 miles.[14]

Oliver, who had met David previously and was sending letters to him from Harmony, wrote the letter to David asking him to come to Harmony to take him and Joseph to Fayette. This was an unusual request, not only because Joseph had never met David, but because it was in late May—prime planting season.

Lucy Mack Smith explained what happened when Oliver's letter arrived.

> David was anxious to respond to the request, but it was one of the most hectic times of the year for a farm family. There were fields to be plowed, planted, and fertilized, and they could not make the trip until the work was done. The day after they received Oliver's letter, David went to plow the fields and discovered that, during the night, five to seven acres had been miraculously plowed by some unknown person. The next day, David went to his field to spread plaster of paris (as a fertilizer). He went to his sister, Catherine Page, to obtain the plaster, but she recounted to him that the previous day she and her children had watched three strangers spread the plaster with great skill and speed. With his

---

[14] Lucy Mack Smith, *History*, 1844-1845, online at http://www.josephsmithpapers.org/paper-summary/lucy-mack-smith-history-1844-1845/100. Emma did not accompany the three men.

fields plowed and fertilized, David was told by his father, "There must be an overruling hand in this, and I think you [had] better go down to Pennsylvania."

David Whitmer related a similar version when he was interviewed by Joseph F. Smith and Orson Pratt in 1878.

> Before I knew Joseph, I had heard about him and the plates from persons who declared they knew he had them, and swore they would get them from him. When Oliver Cowdery went to Pennsylvania, he promised to write me what he should learn about these matters, which he did. He wrote me that Joseph had told him his (Oliver's) secret thoughts, and all he had meditated about going to see him, which no man on earth knew, as he supposed, but himself, and so he stopped to write for Joseph.
>
> Soon after this, Joseph sent for me (D. W.) to come to Harmony to get him and Oliver and bring them to my father's house. I did not know what to do, I was pressed with my work. I had some 20 acres to plow, so I concluded I would finish plowing and then go. I got up one morning to go to work as usual and, on going to the field, found between five and seven acres of my ground had been plowed during the night.
> I don't know who did it; but it was done just as I would have done it myself, and the plow was left standing in the furrow.
> This enabled me to start sooner.[15]

David spent two-and-a-half days to drive a wagon to Harmony and pick them up.

Before leaving Harmony, Joseph gave the plates to a divine messenger. **Lucy Mack Smith** explained:

---

[15] Interview with David Whitmer by Orson Pratt and Joseph F. Smith, September 1878, "Report of Elders Orson Pratt and Joseph F. Smith, *Millennial Star,* 40 (9 Dec 1878):771-74. Online at http://whitmercollege.com/published/interviews/orson-pratt-joseph-f-smith-1878

When Joseph commenced making preparations for the journey, he inquired of the Lord to know in what manner he should carry the plates; his answer was, that he should commit them into the hands of an angel for their safety, and when he should arrive at Mr. Whitmer's, the angel would deliver them up again into his hands.[16]

It is not known how far in advance Joseph gave the plates to the messenger before leaving Harmony, but clearly the messenger had a head start. Naturally, if he was going in the same direction, David's wagon would catch up to him.

If the miraculous farming assistance convinced David and his family that divine providence was involved, another event impressed David with Joseph's prophetic abilities. When he approached Harmony, he found Joseph and Oliver already well on the road to meet him.

David Whitmer told Joseph F. Smith and Orson Pratt what happened:

> When I arrived at Harmony, Joseph and Oliver were coming toward me, and met me some distance from the house. Oliver told me that Joseph had informed him when I started from home, where I had stopped the first night, how I read the sign at the tavern, where I stopped the next night, etc., and that I would be there that day before dinner, and this was why they had come out to meet me; all of which was exactly as Joseph had told Oliver, at which I was greatly astonished.[17]

On the trip back to Fayette, they encountered a man along the road. David offered the man a ride, but the man declined because, as David recalled, the man said he was going to "Cumorah."

---

[16] Lucy Mack Smith, *History*, online at http://www.josephsmithpapers.org/paper-summary/lucy-mack-smith-history-1845/158.

[17] Ibid.

Whatever Happened to the Golden Plates?

David had grown up in the area but had never heard of Cumorah. He said, "This name was something new to me, I did not know what Cumorah meant."

At this time—early June 1829—David had not seen the manuscript. The Book of Mormon wouldn't be published for many months. He could not have known the name *Cumorah* unless Joseph or Oliver had mentioned it. The incident is all the more important because the term *Cumorah* was spoken by a heavenly messenger who was carrying the plates.

In 1878, Orson Pratt and Joseph F. Smith visited David in Richmond, Missouri. He related the event to them and they recorded it in their journals and reported it to President Taylor of the Quorum of the Twelve. This report and others are in Appendix 2.

David Whitmer repeated this account multiple times. Edward Stevenson recorded one version in his journal:

> He also relates a little very interesting incident that occurred in June 1829, David, Oliver, & Joseph were riding from Harmony Pa.—the 2 former in front & Joseph back sitting in the bed on hay or straw David had been down with his team over 100 miles to fetch Joseph up to his mothers to translate the Book of Mormon about 2 ½ days drive. While thus riding an aged looking old man came walking along putting his hand on the wagon bed, he had on his back a knapsack & the strap crossed on his breast he took his handkerchief and wiped his face to remove the sweat as it seemed to them David who was driving his team said to the man will you get up and ride No said he I am only going over to Comorah [sic] & suddenly disappeared they stopped the team at the sudden disappearance of the fine looking stranger he says that they all felt so strangely—that they asked the Prophet to enquire of the Lord who this stranger was. Soon David said they turned around & Joseph looked pale almost transparent & said that was

one of the Nephites and he had the plates of the Book of Mormon in the knapsack—[18]

Edward Stevenson wrote a letter to President John Taylor, dated 7 January 1878, describing his visit with David Whitmer. "He related many very interesting items of seeing one of the Nephites in company of the Prophet & Oliver when Joseph's countenance became almost transparent &c."

Focusing on the name *Cumorah* is important because it raises the important question: why would a divine messenger carrying the plates be heading for Cumorah if he was supposed to be transporting the plates to Fayette?

The Hill Cumorah is about 20 miles northwest of the Whitmer farm near Fayette. When Oliver traveled from the Smith farm near Palmyra to Harmony, he passed through Fayette to visit the Whitmers along the way. Lucy Mack and Joseph Sr. did likewise.

David Whitmer's account doesn't say at what point during the journey between Harmony and Fayette they encountered the messenger. He says they were "traveling along in a clear open place." Although Joseph had told Oliver the details of the trip, we don't have Oliver's notebook and no one recorded the details except to say they were confirmed, so we don't know what route David took. Other known journeys between Harmony and Palmyra went through Colesville, so it is likely David took that route, but alternatives are also possible.

The map below shows the customary route.

---

[18] Edward Stevenson, Diary, 9 February 1886, LDS Church Archives, cited in Lyndon W. Cook, Editor, *David Whitmer Interviews*, p. 181

Whatever Happened to the Golden Plates?

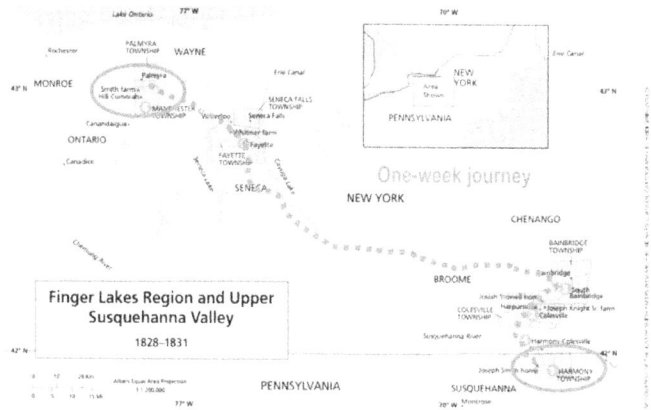

Figure 2 - Customary route Harmony to Palmyra

In this case, the messenger may have had another reason not to ride with David, such as a concern about encountering bandits along the road. That's entirely speculative, of course.

It's also possible that David took a different route to Fayette, such as the one in the map below:

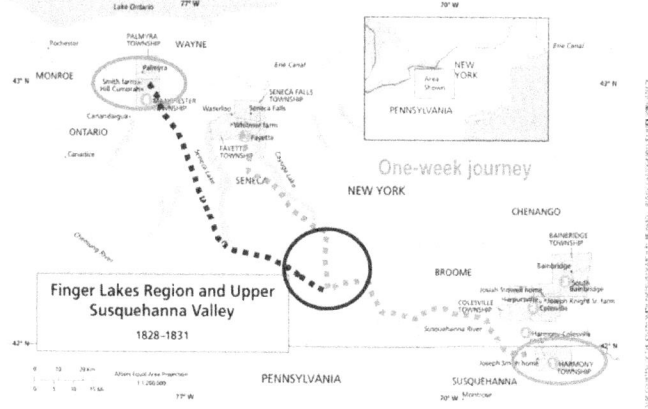

Figure 3 - Alternative route Harmony to Palmyra

In this scenario, they could have met at the point (circled in black) where the messenger would have left the road to travel west of Seneca Lake, possibly a shorter or safer route.

Why would the angel have encountered David? Surely he could have avoided contact. In light of all the miraculous circumstances associated with this trip, it seems likely that the encounter with the messenger was yet another confirmation for David and Oliver that they were engaged in the Lord's work. But it may also have been a teaching moment for Joseph Smith.

Why did Joseph give the plates to the messenger in the first place? Recall that Lucy said "he should commit them into the hands of an angel for their safety." Giving the plates to this messenger would avoid the risk of having them stolen or somehow lost along the way. Joseph had hidden the plates in a barrel of beans to get them to Harmony in the first place. Maybe he didn't have a good hiding place in David's wagon.

In the original version of Lucy Mack Smith's account, she related that

> When he commenced making preparations for his journey he enquired of the Lord in what **manner the plates should be conveyed to their point of destination**. His answer was that he should give himself no trouble about but hasten to waterloo and after he arrived at Mr. Whitmore's house if he would repair immediately to the garden he would receive the plates from the hand of an angel to whose charge they must be committed for their safety.[19]

---

[19] Lucy Mack Smith, *History*, 1844-1845, online at
http://www.josephsmithpapers.org/paper-summary/lucy-mack-smith-history-1844-1845/102. This version is the one she originally dictated. The second version is a fair copy inscribed by Martha and Howard Coray under Lucy's direction. *Lucy's Book*, edited by Lavina Fielding Anderson, (Signature Books 2001) compares the two.

Whatever Happened to the Golden Plates?

Here, Lucy said Joseph asked how "the plates should be conveyed to their destination." She changed that in the second version, as quoted previously, to say he asked "to know in what manner he should carry the plates."

Notice that in the original version, she uses third person singular—*he* commenced, *his* journey, *he* enquired—until she refers to "their point of destination." I think *their* refers to the plates; i.e., Joseph wondered how the plates were going to get to their destination, which was not the same as *his* destination.

I realize this can be read multiple ways, but the shift in pronouns is distinct. It is consistent with the idea that Joseph knew he had finished with the set of plates he originally obtained from Moroni and he wondered what to do with them. In response, the Lord told him not to worry about the plates. The angel would meet him in Fayette (Waterloo) with the plates he would need to complete the work; i.e., the plates of Nephi.

In the later version, Lucy changed this account so that Joseph is now inquiring to know how he should carry the plates. The answer is the same: he is told to give them to an angel. But the connotation is completely different. The latter account implies Joseph thought he was going to keep translating the same set of plates.

It's also strange that Lucy never mentions the encounter with the old man going to Cumorah, even though she relates other details she could only have learned from David Whitmer.

My best explanation of Lucy's account is that she, like the others involved, knew she was not supposed to talk about the repository in the Hill Cumorah. She realized that her first dictation implied the plates had a separate destination from Joseph, so in her second version, she changed the account to conform to the public version of these events; i.e., that there was only one set of plates.

I infer from this that Joseph knew the Harmony plates had a separate destination—*their* destination—but he may not have known what that destination was until he, David and Oliver encountered the messenger along the road and learned from *him* that he was taking the plates to Cumorah.

Recall Stevenson's journal entry of his interview with David Whitmer, quoted above. He said, "Joseph looked pale almost transparent & said that was one of the Nephites and he had the plates of the Book of Mormon in the knapsack."

Why would Joseph turn pale? This always seemed like a strange element of the story to me. Presumably this was the same messenger to whom Joseph had given the plates before they left Harmony. Joseph recognized him, after all. So why the shock? Why turn pale?

I think he turned pale because at that moment he realized, for the first time, that the messenger was going to the repository of Nephite records in Cumorah.

And he realized what was in there.

Joseph and Oliver had translated Mormon 6:6 not long before they left Harmony.

> 6 And it came to pass that when we had gathered in all our people in one to the land of Cumorah, behold I, Mormon, began to be old; and knowing it to be the last struggle of my people, and having been commanded of the Lord that I should not suffer the records which had been handed down by our fathers, which were sacred, to fall into the hands of the Lamanites, (for the Lamanites would destroy them) therefore I made this record out of the plates of Nephi, and **hid up in the hill Cumorah all the records which had been entrusted to me by the hand of the Lord,** save it were these few plates which I gave unto my son Moroni.

It is possible Moroni had previously told Joseph about the repository, but it seems more likely he had not. After all, the very first time Joseph went to the Hill Cumorah, he had struggled with the temptation of knowing the gold would be worth a lot of money. His family was poor and nearly desperate. Sixty pounds of gold in today's valuation is worth over $1 million. Moroni, knowing his thoughts, had told him he was not prepared, spiritually, to receive the plates. It took four years before Joseph was ready to take the plates without immediately selling them or sharing them with his former business partners.

Now, on the trip to Fayette, having left his wife behind and having had to depend on the generosity of Mr. Knight just to survive, he was in even more desperate circumstances than he had been when he first went to Cumorah. Now he had a wife. They had lost a child but hoped for more. He relied on the kindness of the Whitmer family generally, and David specifically, to simply move to a place where he could translate the plates of Nephi in relative peace.

In a word, he was impoverished.

Plus, he had accomplished what he thought was his assignment: he had translated the abridged plates to the last leaf (the Title Page). True, the Lord told him he'd have to translate the plates of Nephi, but he didn't have those plates yet. All he knew was an angel would deliver them once he got to Fayette.

But when the messenger told the group he was going to Cumorah, Joseph apparently realized for the first time what that meant.

The entire records repository of the Nephites was there!

It was one thing to be tempted by a single set of plates—Oliver Cowdery explained at length the thoughts that ran through Joseph's mind on that first trip to Cumorah—but now he realized there were far more than a single set of plates sitting in that hill not far from his father's home.

We don't know whether it was this sudden realization that caused Joseph to turn pale. Maybe he wasn't tempted by the treasure; maybe he was shocked just to know the records were that close. Or that he had a lot more translation work to do. Or that the messenger would so freely mention Cumorah to David and Oliver.

There could be any number of explanations for his turning pale, but under the circumstances, I think it was the realization that the entire repository of Nephite records still existed. And was so close by. And so accessible.

David Whitmer, who observed the Fayette translation only, suggested as much when he said that

> At times when Brother Joseph would attempt to translate he would look into the hat in which the stone was placed, he found he was spiritually blind and could not translate. He told us that his mind dwelt too much on earthly things, and various causes would make him incapable of proceeding with the translation. When in this condition he would go out and pray, and when he became sufficiently humble before God, he could then proceed with the translation.[20]

There could be lots of reasons for Joseph's mind to dwell on earthly things, but the thought of the treasures in the Hill Cumorah was surely one of them.

Some people think the repository of records could not be in the hill in New York because that is not the same as the hill Cumorah/Ramah described in Mormon 6:6. They reject Oliver Cowdery's description in Letter VII (Chapter 6). They think the naming of the hill in New York was a mistake. They say Joseph never used the term Cumorah in connection with that hill; instead, Joseph merely adopted a false tradition started by early Saints.

That conclusion is implausible. Obviously, we can't say Joseph *never* referred to the hill as Cumorah; all we can say is that there is no extant written record of his having done so (prior to D&C 128:20). But his mother, Lucy, said Moroni identified the hill as Cumorah the first time they met.

---

[20] David Whitmer, "Address to All Believers in Christ," p. 30, online at https://archive.org/stream/addresstoallbeli00whit#page/30.

the record is on a side hill on the Hill of Cumorah 3 miles from this place remove the Grass and moss and you will find a large flat stone pry that up and you will find the record under it laying on 4 pillars <of cement>— then the angel left him.[21]

Lucy related another incident when Joseph referred to Cumorah even before he got the plates.[22] Critics say these were "late" memories; i.e., they infer she applied the false tradition retroactively.

The same people claim that David Whitmer also applied the false tradition retroactively when he related the encounter with the old man going to Cumorah. And yet, David emphasized the point that he'd never heard the term before—it was memorable for a good reason. Joseph Smith's surprising reaction of turning "pale, almost transparent" was equally memorable.

In 1881, David gave an interview to the *Kansas City Journal* in which he answered this question:

> "Did Joseph Smith ever relate to you the circumstances of his finding the plates?"
>
> "Yes, he told me that he first found the plates in the year 1823; that during the fall of 1823 he had a vision, an angel appearing to him three times in one night and telling him that there was a record of an ancient people deposited in a hill near his father's house, **called by the ancients `Cumorah,'** situated in the township of Manchester, Ontario County, N. Y. The angel pointed out the exact spot, and, sometime after, he went and found the records or plates deposited in a stone box in the hill, just as had been described to him by the angel.[23]

---

[21] https://www.josephsmithpapers.org/paper-summary/lucy-mack-smith-history-1844-1845/41
[22] http://www.josephsmithpapers.org/paper-summary/lucy-mack-smith-history-1845/111.
[23] David Whitmer Interview, *Kansas City Journal*, 5 June 1881, republished in the *Millennial Star* 42 (1881): 421-23, 437-439, online at http://whitmercollege.com/published/interviews/kansas_city_journal_1881

In this account, David seems to reiterate that Moroni told Joseph the name of the hill at his first meeting. David's statement is consistent with the accounts of all of Joseph's contemporaries, all of whom corroborate Lucy Mack Smith's recollection that it was Moroni himself who identified the hill as Cumorah the first time he met Joseph Smith.

Critics who reject the New York Cumorah nevertheless argue that all of these people were perpetuating a false narrative that originated with an unknown person at an unknown time for an unknown reason.

Others who look at the same evidence adopt the most parsimonious explanation: that Lucy correctly reported that Moroni identified the hill as Cumorah when he first met Joseph Smith because Moroni and the other "ancients" did call it Cumorah.

At any rate, the messenger did bring plates to Fayette. Whether they were the plates of Nephi retrieved from the repository in Cumorah as I believe, or the same ones Joseph had in Harmony as is traditionally understood, Joseph translated them as 1 Nephi, 2 Nephi, Jacob, Enos, Jarom, Omni, and Words of Mormon. We'll explore the significance of the order of translation in Chapter 9.

Before that, let's go back chronologically and take another look at the discovery of the plates (Chapter 6), what we know about them (Chapter 7), and the sealed portion (Chapter 8). Then we'll discuss the witnesses (Chapter 10), the 116 pages (Chapter 11), Mormon's repository (Chapter 12), and the remaining issues.

Whatever Happened to the Golden Plates?

6 The Discovery of the Plates

There are only a few primary accounts of Moroni's visit to Joseph Smith. As Richard Lloyd Anderson observed, "The story of the Book of Mormon translation and visions was produced mainly between the years 1832 and 1839 and hardly grew after that. There is no ongoing mythology of founding, but after those years merely summary testimony based on the narrative record."[24]

All the accounts share the same basic information. Moroni visited Joseph Smith in 1823 and told him about the ancient record—the "gold plates" he, Moroni, had buried in a stone box on the hill in the Town of Manchester. As directed, Joseph went to the hill and found the plates. Because he had been tempted by the material value of the stash of gold, he was not allowed to take the plates at that time.[25]

Joseph visited the site annually, and on the fourth year he was finally allowed to take the plates.

The first account of Moroni's visit was written in the summer of 1832 by Frederick G. Williams, presumably as dictated by Joseph Smith[26] because Joseph wrote most of the

---

[24] Richard Lloyd Anderson, "The Credibility of the Book of Mormon Translators," in Noel B. Reynolds, ed., *Book of Mormon Authorship*, (Religious Studies Center, BYU, 1982): 226.
[25] One contemporaneous source estimated the gold plates, based on a weight of 30 pounds, would be worth about $8,000, equivalent to about $200,000 today, according to inflation calculators. However, 30 pounds of pure gold today is worth over $500,000, and two people estimated the plates weighed twice that much, making them worth over $1 million.
[26] *History*, circa Summer 1832, page 4, online at http://www.josephsmithpapers.org/paper-summary/history-circa-summer-1832/4.

preceding 3 pages in his own handwriting. This brief account says Moroni told Joseph "**there was plates of gold** upon which there was engravings which was engraven by Maroni [sic] & his fathers the servants of the living God in ancient days and deposited by the commandments of God."

This account claims "it was on the 22d day of Sept. AD 1822," instead of 1823.[27]

The second account is contained in Oliver Cowdery's letters about Church history. Letter IV, first published in the *Latter-day Saints' Messenger and Advocate*, February 1835, provides detailed information about Moroni's first visit to Joseph, including his appearance. Letters VII and VIII give us by far the most comprehensive and detailed account of what Moroni told Joseph Smith, not only at the first visit but when Joseph met Moroni on the hill at the site of the plates. Oliver never describes the plates as *gold*.

He establishes the credibility and reliability of his account by explaining that he relied on Joseph's memory. Joseph "continued still to pray... In this situation hours passed unnumbered—how many or how few I know not, neither is he able to inform me, but supposes it must have been eleven or twelve and perhaps later, as the noise and bustle of the family in retiring had long since ceased."

In Letter IV, Oliver seems to speak from personal experience: "It is no easy task to describe the appearance of a messenger from the skies, indeed, I doubt there being an individual clothed with perishable clay, who is capable to do this work."

---

[27] Note 22 in JSP explains, "Later accounts clarify that Moroni first appeared late in the night of 21–22 September 1823. (*JS History*, vol. A-1, 5; Oliver Cowdery, "Letter IV," *LDS Messenger and Advocate*, Feb. 1835, 1:78–79.)"

Whatever Happened to the Golden Plates?

The letters are available online and in my Letter VII book, so I won't reprint them here, but a few excerpts are important to understand the context.

Oliver relates Moroni's words at length, sometimes quoting them and sometimes summarizing them. Notice how he emphasizes Moroni related a history of the aborigines *of this country* and told Joseph that the history *was written and deposited* not far from his house

> He then proceeded and gave a general account of **the promises made to the fathers**, and also gave **a history of the aborigines of this country**, and said they were literal descendants of Abraham. He represented them as once being an enlightened and intelligent people, possessing a correct knowledge of the gospel, and the plan of restoration and redemption. He said **this history was written and deposited not far from that place**, and that it was our brother's privilege, if obedient to the commandments of the Lord, to obtain, and **translate the same by the means of the Urim and Thummim, which were deposited for that purpose with the record**.

Oliver comments on the contents of the sealed portion and Joseph's motivations.

> **A part of the book was sealed**, and was not to be opened yet. The sealed part, said he, **contains the same revelation which was given to John upon the isle of Patmos**, and when the people of the Lord are prepared, and found worthy, then it will be unfolded unto them.
> On the subject of bringing to light the unsealed part of this record, it may be proper to say, that **our brother was expressly informed, that it must be done with an eye single to the glory of God**; if this consideration did not wholly characterize all his proceedings in relation to it, the adversary of truth would overcome him, or at least prevent his making that proficiency in this glorious work which he otherwise would.

In Letter VII, when he reprised Moroni's visit. Oliver dwells on Joseph's thoughts as he made his first trip to the hill.

> **Here was a struggle indeed; for when he calmly reflected upon his errand, he knew that if God did not give, he could not obtain; and again, with the thought or hope of obtaining, his mind would be carried back to its former reflection of poverty, abuse,—wealth, grandeur and ease, until before arriving at the place described, this wholly occupied his desire; and when he thought upon the fact of what was previously shown him, it was only with an assurance that he should obtain and accomplish his desire in relieving himself and friends from want.**
> … Surely, thought he, every man will seize with eagerness, this knowledge, **and this incalculable income will be mine.** Enough to raise the expectations of any one of like inexperience, placed in similar circumstances…
> It is sufficient to say that such were his reflections during his walk of from two to three miles, the distance from his father's house to the place pointed out. **And to use his own words it seemed as though two invisible powers were influencing, or striving to influence his mind**…

Oliver describes the hillside location of the stone-and-cement box Moroni constructed. Then he explains what Joseph found.

> It is sufficient for my present purpose, to know that such is the fact, that in 1823, yes, 1823, a man with whom I have had the most intimate and personal acquaintance, for almost seven years, actually discovered by the vision of God, the plates from which the Book of Mormon, as much as it is disbelieved, was translated!

This statement arguably implies that *all* of the plates from which the Book of Mormon was translated were found in Moroni's box. But notice how carefully Oliver describes what was in the box.

> The manner in which the plates were deposited… From the bottom of the box, or from the breast-plate, arose three small pillars composed of the same description of cement used on the

edges; and upon these three pillars was placed **the record of the children of Joseph, and of a people who left the tower far, far before the days of Joseph, or a sketch of each**, which had it not been for this, and the never failing goodness of God, *we* might have perished in our sins…

Oliver specifies that the record contained "a sketch of each," meaning an abridgment, just as stated in the Title Page. He does not say these plates contained any *original* records of the Nephites or the Jaredites.

After describing the details of the box, Oliver revisits Joseph's mental state at the time.

> … **the mind of man is easily turned,** if it is not held by the power of God through the prayer of faith, and you will remember that I have said that two invisible powers were operating upon his mind during his walk from his residence to Cumorah, and that **the one urging the certainty of wealth and ease in this life, had so powerfully wrought upon him, that the great object so carefully and impressively named by the angel, had entirely gone from his recollection that only a fixed determination to obtain now urged him forward. In this, which occasioned a failure to obtain, at that time, the record, do not understand me to attach blame to our brother: he was young, and his mind easily turned from correct principles, unless he could be favored with a certain round of experience.** And yet, while young, untraditionated and untaught in the systems of the world, he was in a situation to be lead into the great work of God, and be qualified to perform it in due time.

The theme of worldly distractions was a feature of the 1829 trip to Fayette and the subsequent translation at the Whitmer farm, discussed in Chapter 5.

The third account of Moroni's visit and the discovery of the plates is found in Joseph's *Journal*, 1835-1836, which includes an account of the visit of a Robert Mathias, to whom Joseph related his first experience with Moroni.

> When I was about 17 years old I saw another vision of angels, in the night season after I had retired to bed I had not been a sleep… all at once the room was iluminated above the brightness of the sun an angel appeared before me, his hands and feet were naked pure and white, and he stood between the floors of the room, clothed in purity inexpressible, he said unto me I am a messenger sent from God, be faithful and keep his commandments in all things, he told me of a sacred record which **was written on plates of gold,** I saw in the vision the place where they were deposited, **he said the indians, were the literal descendants of Abraham**… also that the Urim and Thumim, was hid up with the record, and that God would give me power to translate it, **with the assistance of this instrument** he then gradually vanished out of my sight, or the vision closed… I went and found the place, where the plates were, according to the direction of the Angel, also saw them, and the angel as before; the powers of darkness strove hard against me, I called on God, the Angel told me that the reason why I could not obtain the plates at this time was because I was under transgression,

This account also alludes to the temptation Joseph struggled with; i.e., the thoughts that the gold plates and artifacts could be worth a lot of money. Again the messenger tells Joseph that the "Indians" were the "literal descendants of Abraham." And again, Joseph found the place where the plates were because the vision was so clear and specific. Joseph refers simply to "a sacred record" without specifying an abridgment or original records.

The fourth account is contained in Joseph Smith's History, 1838-1856.[28] This is the account that was serialized in the 1842

---

[28] Available online at http://www.josephsmithpapers.org/paper-summary/history-1838-1856-volume-a-1-23-december-1805-30-august-1834/5.

Whatever Happened to the Golden Plates?

Times and Seasons and is now in the Pearl of Great Price as Joseph Smith-History.

> 34 He said there was a book deposited, **written upon gold plates,** giving an account of the **former inhabitants of this continent,** and the source from whence they sprang. He also said that the fulness of the everlasting Gospel was contained in it, as delivered by the Savior to the ancient inhabitants;
>
> 35 Also, that there were two stones in silver bows—and these stones, fastened to a breastplate, constituted what is called the Urim and Thummim—deposited with the plates; and the possession and use of these stones were what constituted "seers" in ancient or former times; and that God had prepared them for the purpose of translating the book. …. 41… He quoted many other passages of scripture, and offered many explanations **which cannot be mentioned here.**
>
> 42 Again, he told me, that when I got those plates of which he had spoken—for the time that they should be obtained was not yet fulfilled—**I should not show them to any person; neither the breastplate with the Urim and Thummim; only to those to whom I should be commanded to show them**; if I did I should be destroyed. While he was conversing with me about the plates, the vision was opened to my mind that I could see the place where the plates were deposited, and that so clearly and distinctly that I knew the place again when I visited it.

One striking part of this account is Joseph's statement that the other words of Moroni "cannot be mentioned here." Oliver Cowdery described Moroni's instructions in detail in his eight historical letters. I think Joseph decided Oliver's letters sufficed; after all, Joseph had directed his scribes to copy all eight letters into his personal history back in 1835. Joseph had seen the letters reprinted multiple times, including in the 1841 *Times and Seasons* and *Gospel Reflector*. In this history, Joseph summarizes events, moving quickly toward those not covered by Oliver's letters.

The fifth and final account is the brief recitation in the Wentworth Letter.

> I was also informed concerning **the aboriginal inhabitants of this country,** and shown who they were, and from whence they came; a brief sketch of their origin, progress, civilization, laws, governments, of their righteousness and iniquity, and the blessings of God being finally withdrawn from them as a people was made known unto me: I was also told where there was deposited **some plates on which were engraven an abridgement of the records of the ancient prophets that had existed on this continent.** The angel appeared to me three times the same night and unfolded the same things.

Here, Joseph refers again to the "aboriginal" inhabitants "of this country" as Oliver did in his letters.

Much of the Wentworth letter was edited from an 1840 pamphlet written by Orson Pratt, but this paragraph was not. It completely replaces a much longer section of Pratt's work without using Pratt's language. This suggests Joseph himself wrote it.

The paragraph emphasizes the plates contained an abridgment, without mentioning the existence of original records in the box Moroni prepared. Pratt's equivalent passage refers not to an abridgment but claims Joseph "was informed, that these records contained many sacred revelations pertaining to the gospel of the kingdom, as well as prophecies relating to the great events of the last days."

Pratt's language seems to describe the small plates of Nephi, but Joseph clarified instead that it was the *abridgment* that was in the box.

Whatever Happened to the Golden Plates?

Wentworth Letter Editing

Orson Pratt	Joseph Smith
These records were ~~engraved~~ *engraven* on plates, which had the appearance of gold. Each plate was **six inches wide and** ~~not far from seven by~~ eight inches **long and** ~~in width and length, being~~ not quite as thick as common tin. They were filled on both sides with engravings, in Egyptian characters, and bound together in a volume, as the leaves of a book, ~~and fastened at one edge~~ with three rings running through the whole. This volume was something near six inches in thickness, a part of which was sealed. The characters ~~or letters upon~~ *on* the unsealed part were small, and beautifully engraved. The whole book exhibited many marks of antiquity in its construction, ~~as well as~~ *and* much skill in the art of engraving. With the records was found "a curious instrument, ~~called by~~ *which* the ancients *called* the Urim and Thummim, which consisted of two transparent stones, ~~clear as crystal,~~ set in the *rim* ~~two rims~~ of a bow *fastened to a breastplate*. ~~This was in use, in ancient times, by persons called seers. It was an instrument, by the use which, they received revelation of things distant, or of things past or future.~~"	These records were engraven on plates which had the appearance of gold, each plate was six inches wide and eight inches long and not quite so thick as common tin. They were filled with engravings, in Egyptian characters and bound together in a volume, as the leaves of a book with three rings running through the whole. The volume was something near six inches in thickness, a part of which was sealed. The characters on the unsealed part were small, and beautifully engraved. The whole book exhibited many marks of antiquity in its construction and much skill in the art of engraving. With the records was found a curious instrument which the ancients called "Urim and Thummim," which consisted of two transparent stones set in the rim of a bow fastened to a breastplate.

7 What We Know about the Plates

Because we don't have the plates available for inspection, everything we know about them comes (directly or by hearsay) from the few people who actually saw and handled them. And they told us very little. (Chapter 10 discusses the witnesses.)

The single most authoritative description is probably that given in the 1842 Wentworth letter, both because Joseph Smith signed the letter and because it was edited from Orson Pratt's 1840 pamphlet titled *A[n] Interesting Account of Several Remarkable Visions, and of the Late Discovery of Ancient American Records*. By comparing the two documents, we see that Joseph was very specific about the size of the plates. The adjacent table shows the deletions and insertions to Pratt's original article.[29]

Joseph specified that the plates were six by eight inches, clarifying Pratt's comment that they were "not far" from seven by eight inches. Orson Pratt never saw the plates; he presumably got his information from one or more of the witnesses who did. Martin Harris and David Whitmer both said they were seven inches wide by eight inches in length.

However, an 1830 account has David describing the plates as eight inches square. In an 1881 interview, David said the plates were six by nine inches in size.

The earliest known statement by Harris is from his interview in 1859,[30] and he repeated his statement in 1870.

In 1841, William Smith said the plates were "eight or ten inches long, less in width." He was not one of the official

---

[29] A complete comparison is in my book, *The Editors: Joseph, William and Don Carlos Smith*.
[30] Martin Harris interview, *Tiffany's Monthly*, May 1859, 165, online here: http://www.olivercowdery.com/smithhome/1850s/1859Tiff.htm

witnesses, but he said he saw the plates covered with a cloth and moved his finger over the edges.

His father reportedly told visitors in 1830 that the plates were six inches wide and nine or ten inches long. However, this account was not published until 1870.

These discrepancies in the accounts, together with those discussed below, raise the possibility that the sources were talking about two different sets of plates. It may be that the Three Witnesses and the Eight Witnesses saw two different sets of plates.

To complicate the matter, David Whitmer may have been describing various sets of plates he saw in the Nephite repository in Cumorah, as well as the set he saw as one of the Three Witnesses.

A helpful overview of witness statements is found in an article titled "How Witnesses Described the Gold Plates" by Kirk B. Henrichsen.[31]

The article includes 44 footnotes summarized in the table below. For all the references, refer to his article. Most of the witnesses never described the plates.

Witness descriptions of the plates

Witness	Weight	Plate thickness	Volume thickness
Joseph Smith Jr.		not quite as thick as common tin	something near six inches
Martin Harris	40-60 lbs; 40 or 50 pounds	Thickness of plates of tin	about four inches thick
Martin Harris	Heft of lead or gold	Thin leaves of gold	

---

[31] The article is available online here:
http://scholarsarchive.byu.edu/cgi/viewcontent.cgi?article=1267&context=j bms.

Whatever Happened to the Golden Plates?

Martin Harris	My daughter said they were about as much as she could lift		
William Smith	About 60 lbs., much heavier than a stone and very much heavier than wood	We could raise the leaves this way (raising a few leaves of a Bible before him)	
William Smith		Thickness of a pane of glass	Five or six inches high
Emma Smith	I moved them from place to place on the table.	Pliable like thick paper, would rustle with a metallic sound when the edges were moved by the thumb.	
Catherine Smith	"hefted those plates and found them very heavy."		
David Whitmer		About as thick as parchment	
Joseph Smith Sr.	30 pounds		1/2 inch, contains the spectacles

The outlier in these accounts is Joseph Smith Sr.'s description. The full description was not published until May 1870, but was based on an interview in 1830.

> In answer to our question, as to what it was that Joseph had thus obtained, he said it consisted of a set of gold plates, about **six inches wide, and nine or ten inches long**. They were in the form of a book, **half an inch thick**, but were not bound at the back, like our books, but were held together by several gold rings, in such a way that the plates could be opened similar to a book. **Under the first plate, or lid, he found a pair of spectacles**,

about one and a half inches longer than those used at the present day, the eyes not of glass, but of diamond.[32]

The interview contains several obvious errors, but also some elements that corroborate other accounts, so it should not be dismissed entirely. Perhaps Joseph's father said half a *foot* thick (instead of half an inch) and the interviewer wrote two marks instead of one (" instead of '). Possibly the spectacles were in a compartment that appeared to David Whitmer to be as "solid as wood," which may also have made it look like half the volume was sealed.

Sealed portion. In the Wentworth Letter, Joseph simply states of the record that "a part of which was sealed."

The sealed portion has generated much discussion, based on a variety of descriptions. Chapter 8 looks at this aspect of the plates in more detail.

Rings. David Whitmer and Martin Harris both said the plates were fastened with three rings. Whitmer said they were shaped like a capital D and were gold. Harris said they were silver. John Whitmer said the plates "were hung" on rings. Orson Pratt added that a rod could be passed through the rings "as a greater convenience for carrying them."

Engravings. The Wentworth letter refers to "Egyptian characters" on the unsealed part that were small and beautifully engraved. John Whitmer said "there were fine engravings on both sides." William Smith related that the "characters… were cut into the plates with some sharp instrument." Orson Pratt,

---

[32] "Interview with the Father of Joseph Smith, *Historical Magazine* (2d series), Volume 7, May 1870, online at
https://en.wikisource.org/w/index.php?title=Historical_Magazine_%28second_series%29/Volume_7/May_1870/Interview_with_the_Father_of_Joseph_Smith&oldid=314358.

who never saw the plates, said the engravings were "stained with a black, hard stain, so as to make the letters more legible and easier to be read."

Martin Harris said Joseph found "the plates of gold upon which was recorded in Arabic, Chaldaic, Syriac, and Egyptian, the Book of Life, or the Book of Mormon."

Some years after the visit of Martin Harris, Charles Anthon provided written statements that claimed the "characters were arranged in columns, like the Chinese mode of writing.... Greek, Hebrew and all sorts of letters, more or less distorted... were intermingled with sundry delineations of half moons, stars, and other natural objects, and the whole ended in a rude representation of the Mexican zodiac."

Joseph's father is reported to have said "On the next page were representations of all the masonic implements, as used by masons at the present day. The remaining pages were closely written over in characters of some unknown tongue, the last containing the alphabet of this unknown language. Joseph, not being able to read the characters, made a copy of some of them, which he showed to some of the most learned men of the vicinity."

Obviously these descriptions don't match. They seem much different from the well-known "Caractors" document that John Whitmer may have copied from an original transcription made by Joseph Smith from the plates. This contradictory evidence tells us little about what the characters on the plates actually looked like.

What about the Egyptian characters?

The Wentworth letter refers to Egyptian characters, but it is referring to the plates of the original Book of Mormon. What about the small plates of Nephi? Could they have been written, in whole or in part, in Hebrew?

Because Moroni said he wrote in "reformed Egyptian," scholars have long assumed that all of the plates Joseph translated were written in this language.

Moroni explained:

> 32 And now, behold, we have written this record according to our knowledge, in the characters which are called among us the reformed Egyptian, being handed down and altered by us, according to our manner of speech.
>
> 33 And if our plates had been sufficiently large we should have written in Hebrew; but the Hebrew hath been altered by us also; and if we could have written in Hebrew, behold, ye would have had no imperfection in our record.

This passage is the only mention of "reformed Egyptian" in the entire text. The title page refers only to the abridgments written by Mormon and Moroni (and Moroni's sealing). They were the only authors of the "original" Book of Mormon; they are the ones of whom Moroni wrote: "we have written this record."

Nephi begins his record by stating, "I make a record in the language of my father, which consists of the learning of the Jews and the language of the Egyptians" (1 Nephi 1:2). Does this mean he, too, wrote in Egyptian?

As the *Encyclopedia of Mormonism* points out, we simply don't have enough information to tell.

> It is unknown whether Nephi, Mormon, or Moroni wrote Hebrew in modified Egyptian characters or inscribed their plates in both the Egyptian language and Egyptian characters or whether Nephi wrote in one language and Mormon and Moroni, who lived some nine hundred years later, in another. The mention of "characters" called "reformed Egyptian" tends to support the hypothesis of Hebrew in Egyptian script. Although Nephi's observation (1 Ne.

1:2) is troublesome for that view, the statement is ambiguous and inconclusive for both views.[33]

That said, it is unlikely that the writings of Isaiah that Nephi quoted were recorded on the brass plates in Egyptian characters.

> Egyptian was widely used in Lehi's day, but because poetic writing are skewed in translation, because prophetic writings were generally esteemed as sacred, and because Hebrew was the language of the Israelites in the seventh century B.C., it would have been unusual for the writings of Isaiah and Jeremiah-substantially preserved on the brass plates (1 Ne. 5:13;19:23)-to have been translated from Hebrew into a foreign tongue at this early date. Thus, Hebrew portions written in Hebrew script, Egyptian portions in Egyptian script, and Hebrew portions in Egyptian script are all possibilities.[34]

King Benjamin told his sons that Lehi could read the engravings because he had "been taught in the language of the Egyptians" (Mosiah 1:4), suggesting that the plates of brass were actually kept in that language. But for the reasons mentioned above, it seems unlikely that the words of Isaiah would have been written in Egyptian characters, particularly when Joseph translated them nearly word-for-word like the King James version, which was translated from Hebrew.

It is possible that a different script on the small plates of Nephi—say Hebrew instead of reformed Egyptian—may explain some of the differences in the translation accounts between Harmony and Fayette. It's a topic worthy of further study.

Number of plates. We don't know how many plates there were in either set of plates, but some estimates have been

---

[33] Brian D. Stubbs, "Book of Mormon Language," *Encyclopedia of Mormonism*, online at http://eom.byu.edu/index.php/Book_of_Mormon_Language.
[34] Ibid.

developed. One early writer claimed the plates were 1/8 of an inch thick so that only 8 plates per inch were possible. Such a thickness would contradict the statements of Emma Smith and William Smith that they ran their fingers up the plates and they rustled like thick paper. Other statements that the plates were like a thick parchment make more sense, but again, it could be that these discrepancies involved two different sets of plates.

The witnesses said there were engravings on both sides of each plate. One LDS artist who works with metal concluded that a sheet of brass 12 thousandths of an inch (0.012") thick is sufficient to allow engraving on both sides, while retaining the flexibility needed to account for the rustling sound multiple witnesses described.

That thickness would allow as much as 80 plates per inch, tightly bound. Loosely bound, if the plates were uneven, could mean far fewer plates per inch, possibly as few as 40 per inch.

An influential estimate of the number of plates was developed by Jann Sjodahl, published in the *Improvement Era* in April 1923.[35] He used the figure of six inches for the thickness of the volume of plates, 8" x 7" for dimensions, and Orson Pratt's statement that 2/3 of the plates were sealed. That left two inches of plates, each about the thickness of tin.

Sjodahl had a friend translate fourteen pages of the American text into Hebrew, using the "square letters in which the Hebrew Bibles now are printed." The text fit on a sheet 7 x 8 inches, albeit with very small characters that would probably be difficult to engrave on metal plates. By Sjodahl's calculations, the entire text could be written on 21 plates, front and back. Much larger characters would still allow the text to be engraved on 48 plates.

---

[35] J. M. Sjodahl, "The Book of Mormon Plates," *Improvement Era*, Vol. 26, No. 6 (April 1923), online at
https://archive.org/stream/improvementera2606unse#page/541/mode/1up.

Of course, this is all speculative, but it shows there is plenty of leeway to accommodate various theories.

The *Historical Magazine* interview of Joseph Smith Sr., cited above, also relates this:

> Under the first plate, or lid, he found a pair of spectacles, about one and a half inches longer than those used at the present day, the eyes not of glass, but of diamond.

The claim that there was a container for the interpreters inside the bound plates might explain some of the different descriptions of the plates. Maybe the plates, cover to cover, were six inches thick, as most witnesses said, but two or three inches was taken up by the compartment for the interpreters. This would explain Martin Harris' statement that the plates were four inches thick and why David Whitmer said the sealed portion was "solid as wood." He may have assumed the compartment was the sealed portion.

Moroni told Joseph there were "two stones in silver bows deposited with the plates" (Joseph Smith-History 1:35). This has normally been understood to mean the interpreters were loose in the stone box, but would such a delicate, important instrument be left loose? Perhaps "with the plates" meant inside this compartment.

When he removed the stone, Joseph said "I looked in, and there indeed did I behold the plates, the Urim and Thummim, and the breastplate." This implies the spectacles were loose, but it's also possible Joseph opened the lid to see them. He said he could not remove the objects, but that doesn't preclude him from opening the lid.

Lucy Mack Smith related that when Lucy Harris came to Harmony insisting on seeing the plates, Joseph "removed both the breast-plate and the Record from the house."[36] She didn't mention the spectacles, which suggests they may have been in the compartment in the plates.

Oliver Cowdery described the stone box in detail in Letter VIII. He said the breast-plate was on the bottom. From there "arose three small pillars" upon which was placed the record. He didn't mention the interpreters.

---

[36] Anderson, *Lucy's Book*, p. 405.

8 Sealed plates

Joseph Smith and others said a portion of the plates were sealed, meaning he could not view them.

The existence of sealed plates refutes the idea that Joseph didn't actually use the plates when he translated them. This point should be obvious, but the theory persists that all he did was read the words that appeared on a seer stone (the stone-in-the-hat theory, or SITH narrative). I think that theory is a mistake.

Several witnesses, as well as Joseph, mentioned that a portion of the plates were sealed. Nephi, describing the plates more than 2,000 years in advance, said they would be sealed (2 Nephi 27: 7-17). Moroni said he was required to seal a portion (Ether 3: 23-28; 4:5; 5:1).

If Joseph didn't use the plates—if he merely read words off the stone in the hat—sealing them would be no impediment to reading them. The stone, according to the theory, did everything.

This is an important point because if Joseph didn't actually use the plates during the translation, it wouldn't matter if he had one or two sets. Or no plates at all.

The five references in D&C 10 to the "plates of Nephi" would have been meaningless as well. Verse 41, for example, tells Joseph "you shall **translate the engravings** which are on **the plates of Nephi**, down even till you come to the reign of king Benjamin, or until you come to that which you have translated, which you have retained."

The Lord told Joseph to translate the engravings, not merely read the words off a stone in a hat. D&C 10 does not mention a sealed portion; instead, Joseph is to stop the translation once he reaches the reign of king Benjamin.

The Eight Witnesses wrote that Joseph showed them the plates "and as many of the leaves as the said Smith has translated we did handle with our hands." However, they never mentioned a sealed portion. This opens the possibility that they saw and handled the plates of Nephi, and that Joseph showed them the portion he translated, "down" to the reign of king Benjamin," but that they did not see any sealed portion.

We know relatively little about the sealed portion. In the Wentworth letter, Joseph gave his most complete description of the plates he found in the box. All he said about the sealed portion was "**a part of which was sealed.**"[37] (emphasis added)

In 1878, David Whitmer was interviewed by P. Wilhelm Poulson. Poulson's report was published in the *Deseret Evening News* on 16 August 1878.

> "I—Did the angel turn all the leaves before you as you looked on it?
> "He—No, not all, only that part of the book which was not sealed, and **what there was sealed appeared as solid to my view as wood**.
> "I—How many of the plates were sealed?
> "He—**About the half of the book was sealed**. Those leaves which were not sealed, about the half of the first part of the book, were numerous, and the angel turned them over before our eyes."

An 1881 *Chicago Times* report claimed "The plates which Mr. Whitmer saw were in the shape of a tablet, fastened with three rings, **about one-third of which appeared to be loose, in plates, the other solid**, **but with perceptible marks where the plates seemed to be sealed,** and the guide that pointed it out to Smith very impressively reminded him that the loose

---

[37] *Times and Seasons*, 1 March 1842. Available online at https://www.churchofjesuschrist.org/study/ensign/2002/07/the-wentworth-letter?lang=eng. Note: the version in the lesson manual *Presidents of the Church: Joseph Smith* was edited to omit important parts of the letter, so I don't recommend using that version.

plates alone were to be used; the sealed portion was not to be tampered with."[38]

An 1888 newspaper article reports that David Whitmer said "**A large portion of the leaves were so securely bound** that **it was impossible to separate them**, but upon the loose leaves were engraved hieroglyphics which were unintelligible to any person who had seen them."[39]

William Smith was interviewed by James Murdock in 1841. "The pages which he was not to translate were **found to be sealed together, so that he did not even read them or learn their contents.**"[40]

Lucy Mack Smith said, "I have myself seen and handled the golden plates; they are about eight inches long, and six wide; **some of them are sealed together and are not to be opened, and some of them are loose**."[41]

Orson Pratt, who never saw the plates, nevertheless provided a description. "[W]hen the Book of Mormon was translated from the plates, **about two-thirds were sealed up**, and Joseph was commanded not to break the seal; that part of the record was hid up. The plates which were sealed contained an account of those things shewn unto the brother of Jared." [42]

Two explanations help account for the differences in these accounts. First, the witnesses may be describing two different sets of plates, each with sealed portions. Second, as mentioned in the previous chapter, the Harmony plates may have had a compartment for the interpreters that appeared "solid as wood" when viewed from a distance.

---

[38] David Whitmer to the Chicago Times, 14 October 1881, in *David Whitmer Interviews*, Cook, ed. p. 75.
[39] David Whitmer to the Chicago Tribune, 24 January 1888, in *David Whitmer Interviews*, Cook, ed. p. 221.
[40] William Smith interview with James Murdock, 18 April 1841 (EMD 1, p. 477)
[41] OTH, #106, p. 163
[42] *Deseret News*, July 23, 1856, 154

9 The Translation of the Plates

In this chapter, we're focusing on two aspects of the translation of the Book of Mormon:
(a) the order of translation and
(b) the use of the plates.

Many readers are not aware that the Book of Mormon, was not dictated in the order it appears today. The last section Joseph dictated, from 1 Nephi through Words of Mormon, appears at the front of the book. He dictated that section in Fayette, New York, in June 1829.

From November 1828 through May, 1829, Joseph dictated Mosiah through Moroni, in Harmony, Pennsylvania, a chronology covered in section 9(a) below.

Joseph's account of *obtaining* the plates is well known, but his *actual use* of the plates is a matter of debate among scholars who disagree about whether Joseph actually used the plates when he translated. We'll discuss that question in section 9(b) below.

At the Church conference in Ohio in October 1831 mentioned in Chapter 1 above, Joseph said "that it was not intended to tell the world all the particulars of the coming forth of the Book of Mormon, & also said that it was not expedient for him to relate these things &c."[43] While the phrase "coming forth" presumably includes the translation, it encompasses more than that.

Why should we care about the "particulars" if Joseph said it was not expedient for him to relate them?

The obvious answer is that our current circumstances present different problems than Joseph faced (just as

---

[43] *Minutes*, 25-26 October 1831, available online at
http://www.josephsmithpapers.org/paper-summary/minutes-25-26-october-1831/4.

circumstances changed after 1831, leading Joseph and Oliver to gradually document the events involved with "the coming forth of the Book of Mormon" as we discussed in Chapter 1).

When Joseph and Oliver were alive, believers accepted their unequivocal teaching about the Hill Cumorah in New York. Now, in 2022, many Latter-day Saint scholars explicitly *reject* that teaching. The two-Cumorahs theory has come to prevail in the Church, as I discussed in the Introduction.

When Joseph and Oliver were alive, believers accepted their explanation that Joseph translated the plates by means of the Urim and Thummim. Now, in 2022, scholars reject that teaching and claim Joseph didn't even use the plates or the Urim and Thummim. They teach instead that he merely read words that appeared on a stone in the hat (SITH).

In my view, the details of the coming forth of the Book of Mormon help to restore the credibility and reliability of Joseph and Oliver. Therefore, knowing more about the particulars has become important.

9a The order of translation

When Martin Harris acted as scribe in 1828, Joseph dictated the abridged Book of Lehi from the plates—the 116 pages that Harris later lost. As a consequence, Joseph temporarily forfeited the plates and the interpreters. After he received them back in September 1828, he resumed the translation in November with Emma as scribe. Because the Mosiah section of the Original Manuscript was ruined by water in Nauvoo,[44] we cannot tell for sure what Emma recorded, but it seems likely she recorded most

---

[44] The extant Original Manuscript is missing everything from Enos 1:14 through Alma 10:31. See *Revelations and Translations, Volume 5: Original Manuscript of the Book of Mormon*, The Joseph Smith Papers (Church Historian's Press: Salt Lake City, UT 2021): 203-205.

or all of Mosiah because they worked on the translation intermittently for five months before Oliver Cowdery arrived in April 1829.[45]

> The work of translating the tablets consumed **about eight months**, Smith acting as the seer and **Oliver Cowdery, Smith's wife, and Christian Whitmer,** brother of David, performing the duties of amanuenses [scribe], in whose handwriting the original manuscript now is.[46]

Oliver and Joseph translated the abridged plates at Harmony during April and May 1829 and then moved to Fayette to translate the plates of Nephi during June 1829. We can tell this because the Original Manuscript contains 1 Nephi with the handwriting of Christian and John Whitmer, who never went to Harmony.

Thus, after Martin lost the 116 pages, Joseph continued translating Mosiah and continued through Moroni before translating 1 Nephi through Words of Mormon. In fact, page 117—a portion Joseph had translated but was not included in the 116 pages Martin took—was probably the first chapter of Mosiah, a point I'll discuss later in this section.)

This order of translation might seem counterintuitive because the Book of Mormon currently starts with 1 Nephi, but recall that the first section of the Book of Mormon, 1 Nephi through Words of Mormon, translated from the plates of Nephi, replaces the lost 116 pages.

The current edition follows the chronological order of events in the text, *not* the chronological order of translation. In

---

[45] See Chapter 1 in, Jonathan Neville, *A Man That Can Translate* (Salt Lake City, Utah) 2021.
[46] Vol. XLV, *The Chicago Daily Tribune*, Thursday, December 17, 1885, discussed in Chapter 5. Oliver, Emma and Christian were scribes at the Whitmer home in Fayette. David could also observe Emma's scribal work on the manuscript Joseph brought from Harmony.

fact, the Title Page which is at the beginning of the text today was translated from the very last leaf of the abridged plates.

The generally accepted order of translation is described in an article in *BYU Studies*:[47]

Order of Translation

Mormon's Abridgment from the Large Plates of Nephi:
Lehi (the lost 116 pages), Mosiah, Alma, Helaman, 3 Nephi, 4 Nephi, Mormon 1–7

Moroni's Writings and Abridgment:
Mormon 8–9, Ether, Moroni

Small Plates of Nephi:
1 Nephi, 2 Nephi, Jacob, Enos, Jarom, Omni, Words of Mormon (at least 1–11)[48]

I agree with this order of translation, except I think the reason the small plates were translated last is that they were a separate set of plates that Joseph didn't have until he arrived in Fayette.

Some people have proposed that Joseph and Oliver started translating 1 Nephi in late May, which would negate my theory. In my view, the evidence shows they started on 1 Nephi only after they arrived at the Whitmer home in Fayette in June.

I offer five reasons.

1. Handwriting of scribes. The handwriting on the original manuscript shows that Oliver Cowdery acted as scribe for 1 Nephi 2:2 through 1 Nephi 3:7, where John Whitmer took

---

[47] Jack M. Lyon and Kent R. Minson, "When Pages Collide: Dissecting the Words of Mormon," *BYU Studies*, 51:4 (2012), available online at https://byustudies.byu.edu/content/when-pages-collide-dissecting-words-mormon.

[48] This parenthetical about verses 1-11 is my addition and we'll discuss it in Chapter 11

over. (The leaf from the original manuscript that would contain 1 Nephi 1:1-2:1 is missing.)

When David drove Joseph and Oliver to his father's home in Fayette in June 1829, Joseph met John Whitmer for the first time. Therefore, these verses must have been translated in Fayette.

You can see the actual pages with the respective handwriting in the Joseph Smith Papers at this link: http://www.josephsmithpapers.org/paper-summary/book-of-mormon-manuscript-excerpt-circa-june-1829-1-nephi-22b-318a/2.

Only about 28 percent of the original manuscript has survived. (Most of it was damaged by water after Joseph placed it in the cornerstone of the Mansion House in Nauvoo.) Dean Jessee identified the handwriting for most of the verses.[49] All of the handwriting is Oliver Cowdery's except for portions of 1 Nephi that are in the handwriting of John Whitmer and, presumably, Christian Whitmer.[50]

In addition to Emma Smith, Samuel Smith and Martin Harris may have briefly acted as scribes in February and March 1829, but their handwriting doesn't appear on the parts of the Original Manuscript we have now. Beginning in April, Oliver Cowdery took over as scribe through the end of Moroni while in Harmony. When he and Joseph arrived in Fayette, they started with the plates of Nephi.

The Fayette portion of the Original Manuscript uses a different type of paper from what was used in Harmony.

---

[49] Dean C. Jessee, "The Original Book of Mormon Manuscript," *BYU Studies* 10:3, (Spring 1970), cited in the Gospel Topics Essay on the translation and available online here: https://byustudies.byu.edu/content/original-book-mormon-manuscript.

[50] See *Revelations and Translations, Volume 5: Original Manuscript of the Book of Mormon.*

2. Joseph Knight. Joseph Knight was an early supporter of Joseph Smith and he apparently thought they finished the translation in Harmony.

In his *Reminiscences*, he writes that after Oliver arrived in Harmony and began acting as scribe, Oliver and Joseph ran out of supplies:

> Now Joseph and Oliver Came up to see me if I Could help him to some provisons, [they] having no way to Buy any. But I was to Cattskill. But when I Came home my folks told me what Joseph wanted. But I had ingaged to go to Catskill again the next Day and I went again and I Bought a Barral of Mackrel and some lined paper for writing. And when I Came home I Bought some nine or ten Bushels of grain and five or six Bushels taters [potatoes] and a pound of tea, and I went Down to see him and they ware in want. Joseph and Oliver ware gone to see if they Could find a place to work for provisions, But found none. They returned home and found me there with provisions, and they ware glad for they ware out. Their familey Consisted of four, Joseph and wife, Oliver and his [Joseph's] Brother Samuel. **Then they went to work and had provisions enough to Last till the translation was Done.** Then he agreed with Martin Harris to print. They therefore agreed with E Grandin to Print five thousand Coppies which was Printed and Bound at Palmiry in the Spring of 1830.[51] (emphasis mine)

Knight's account is brief, but he does not mention the move to Fayette. He provided Joseph and Oliver enough provisions "to last till the translation was done," which suggests he thought the translation was finished there in Harmony. Of course, Knight could have meant he gave them enough provisions to enable them to translate until David Whitmer arrived to take them to Fayette, where they completed the translation. But it could also mean that Knight thought he gave them enough

---

[51] Dean Jessee, "Joseph Knight's Recollection of Early Mormon History," *BYU Studies* 17:1 (1977), available online at
http://publications.mi.byu.edu/fullscreen/?pub=970&index=1.

provisions to finish the translation, which suggests they finished translating the plates they had—except for the sealed portion—while they were in Harmony. In other words, they didn't have the plates of Nephi when they were in Harmony.

3. The organization of the plates. The way the plates were organized suggests the plates of Nephi *were not in Moroni's stone box*.

The plates are typically depicted with the "small plates of Nephi" stacked on top of the "large plates of Nephi," with the Words of Mormon sandwiched between them. The diagram below is an example from BYU Studies:[52]

The diagram helps students place the original sources in today's published edition, but the structure depicted does not match the historical record.[53]

---

[52] https://byustudies.byu.edu/charts/2-13-book-mormon-plates-and-records.
[53] Note that the diagram is oriented the way we read books, turning pages from right to left with the unread text on the right side of the ring binders. The actual plates would have been reversed, with the unread text on the left side of the ring binders.

Book of Mormon Plates and Records

If, as is generally assumed, Mormon added the plates of Nephi (translated into what is now 1 Nephi through the Words of Mormon) to his abridgement, where did he put them?

(The traditional understanding is based on Mormon's observation in Words of Mormon that he "put them with the remainder of my record." I will address that and other aspects of the Words of Mormon in Chapter 11 below.)

There are four possibilities for the placement of the plates of Nephi, but none are satisfactory. They could have been (i) at the beginning, (ii) in the middle, (iii) at the end of the loose plates (before the sealed portion) or (iv) after the sealed portion.

(i) With Martin Harris as scribe, Joseph translated the Book of Lehi first (which became the lost 116 pages). They presumably started translating at the beginning of the plates. This means that the plates of Nephi were not at the beginning of the record, contrary to the depiction in the diagram.

(ii) The plates of Nephi could not have been in the middle of the record. After the manuscript was lost, Joseph resumed

Whatever Happened to the Golden Plates?

the translation with the Book of Mosiah. Chapter 1 of the current Book of Mosiah appears to have been the original Chapter 3.[54] Joseph and Oliver translated the record from that point through the end of Moroni. If Mormon had inserted the plates of Nephi *prior* to the Book of Mosiah, the translation would have been included in the 116 pages. If Mormon had inserted the plates of Nephi at the end of his own Book of Mormon, then Joseph would have translated that before he got to Moroni's additions to his father's book (Mormon 8-9). The plates of Nephi don't fit anywhere within Mormon's abridgement.

(iii) Mormon could not have attached them to the end of the loose plates because it was Moroni, not Mormon, who completed the record (Mormon 8-9, Ether, and Moroni).

(iv) Mormon could not have attached them after the sealed portion for the same reason as (iii).

One could argue that *Moroni* attached the plates of Nephi instead of Mormon. Maybe Mormon attached them somewhere, but then Moroni moved them to another place on the three-ring binder. Moroni could have attached them at the end of his own book, or after the sealed portion.

However, *Moroni never mentioned the plates of Nephi.*

His father commanded him to write "but few things." (Mormon 8:1), which is what we now know as Mormon 8 and 9. Later, Moroni added his abridgment of the Jaredite record (Ether) and "supposed not to have written more." (Moroni 1:1). Because he did not perish as he expected, he wrote his own short

---

[54] Scholars think this because (i) the Book of Mosiah begins with the account of King Benjamin, (ii) it has no introductory comments, and (iii) the first page of the printer's manuscript originally read Chapter III. On the Printer's Manuscript, Oliver crossed out two of the Roman numerals so it now reads Chapter I.

book of ten chapters, including three long quotations of Mormon's writings, before closing his book and the overall record with his stirring final verse (Moroni 10:34).

But again, he said nothing about the plates of Nephi.

If Moroni somehow attached the plates of Nephi after his own book, or after the sealed portion, Joseph and Oliver would have translated the small plates of Nephi before they considered going back to the beginning to re-translate the Book of Lehi. But as we'll see in number 6 below, D&C 10 instructs Joseph not to retranslate the Book of Lehi, but instead to translate the plates of Nephi. If the plates of Nephi were in the record he had in Harmony, the direction in D&C 10 would have been pointless.

There is no practical physical place for the plates of Nephi in the abridgement Joseph received from Moroni.

4. The title page. Notice that the title page *does not mention the plates of Nephi as part of the record*. This is a critical point.

In his history, Joseph explained the origin of the Title Page. Here is the transcript from the Joseph Smith Papers:[55]

> I wish also to mention here, that the Title Page of the Book of Mormon **is a literal translation**, taken from the **very last leaf, on the left hand side of the collection or book of plates, which contained the record which has been translated**; the language of the whole running same as all Hebrew writing in general; and that, said Title Page is not by any means a modern composition either of mine or of any other man's who has lived or does live in this generation. Therefore, in order to correct an error which generally exists concerning it, I give below that part of the Title Page of the English Version of the Book of Mormon, **which is a genuine and literal translation of the Title Page of the Original Book of Mormon**, as recorded on the plates.

---

[55] *History*, 1838-1856, volume A-1, online at http://www.josephsmithpapers.org/paper-summary/history-1838-1856-volume-a-1-23-december-1805-30-august-1834/40.

Whatever Happened to the Golden Plates?

> The Book of Mormom [sic]
> **An account written by the hand of Mormon, upon plates, Taken from the plates of Nephi.**
>
> Wherefore it is **an abridgement of the record of the people of Nephi,** and also of the Lamanites; written to the Lamanites, who are a remnant of the house of Israel; and also to Jew and Gentile: written by way of commandment, and also by the spirit of prophecy and of revelation.
>
> **Written, and sealed up, and hid up unto the Lord, that they might not be destroyed**; to come forth by the gift and power of God **unto the interpretation thereof**: sealed by the hand of Moroni, and hid up unto the Lord, to come forth in due time by the way of Gentile; **the interpretation thereof** by the gift of God.
>
> **An abridgement taken from the book of Ether, also**; which is a record of the people of Jared; who were scattered at the time the Lord confounded the language of the people when they were building a tower to get to Heaven: which is to shew unto the remnant of the house of Israel what great things the Lord hath done for their fathers; and that they may know the Covenants of the Lord, that they are not cast off forever; and also to the convincing of <the> Jew and Gentile that Jesus is the Christ, the Eternal God, manifesting himself unto all nations. And now if there are faults, they are the mistakes of men; wherefore condemn not the things of God, that ye may be found spotless at the judgement seat of Christ.
> (The remainder <(of the Title page)> is of course, modern).

The Title Page was obviously written by Moroni; he said he sealed it, and Mormon would not have known about Moroni's abridgement of the book of Ether. (Some scholars propose that Mormon himself wrote the first paragraph of the Title Page. That's possible, but not significant either way.)

Moroni lists the contents of the plates he deposited:

(i) An account written by the hand of Mormon, upon plates, Taken from the plates of Nephi. Wherefore it is an abridgement of the record of the people of Nephi.

(ii) An abridgement taken from the book of Ether, also.

(iii) His own comments at the end of his father's book and in his own Book of Moroni, which he refers to when he writes "sealed by the hand of Moroni."

But nowhere does Moroni mention the original plates of Nephi written by Nephi and his successors down to Amaleki.

Instead, the title page *excludes* any original plates from the record Moroni sealed and hid up unto the Lord.

Joseph Smith provided his explanation of the title page "in order to correct an error which generally exists concerning it." The obvious error was people thinking Joseph composed the book because he was listed as "author & Proprietor" on the copyright application, a statutory requirement. Explaining that the Title Page itself was translated from the last leaf of the plates shows he was not actually the "author" in the sense of the originator of the work.

Nevertheless, the Title Page does not mention the material translated in Fayette.

Copyright. Although Joseph apparently did not fully comply with the requirements of the federal Copyright Act,[56] he did apply for a copyright. It was important that the copyright include the Fayette translation even though it was not described by the Title Page. This could be a reason why there is no record of Joseph clarifying that the Title Page pertained to the plates he found in the box, but *not* to the plates of Nephi which he translated separately in Fayette. He needed the Title Page to cover the entire book as published.

---

[56] Nathaniel H. Wadsworth, Copyright Laws and the 1830 Book of Mormon, *BYU Studies*, 45:3 (2006), online at
https://byustudies.byu.edu/content/copyright-laws-and-1830-book-mormon.

Whatever Happened to the Golden Plates?

The timing of the copyright application supports the idea that there were two sets of plates.

The court clerk in Utica, New York, certified that Joseph Smith Junior "deposited" the "title of a book" on June 11, 1829, in Utica, New York.[57] Although the clerk wrote the title page in longhand on his certification, he copied it from a printed copy because Joseph had to submit a *printed* copy of the title as part of the application.[58] Utica is about 100 miles from both Harmony and Fayette. It is not known where the Title Page was printed, except that it probably wasn't printed by Grandin in Palmyra. It could have been printed anywhere between Harmony and Fayette. Binghamton had printers during this time frame, for example. It is also not known whether Joseph mailed the printed copy to the court or sent someone to hand deliver it. Either way, the Title Page had to be translated, printed, and submitted far enough in advance to arrive at Utica no later than June 11. This suggests Joseph translated the Title Page before he gave the plates to the messenger before leaving Harmony for the two-and-a-half day trip to Fayette.

The Title Page was on the last leaf of the plates. This means it had to be the last leaf of the plates he translated in Harmony, because in early June he started at the beginning of the plates of Nephi in Fayette. He wouldn't reach the end of those plates until the end of June.

The limited nature of the Title Page has not gone unnoticed. For example, John Tvedtnes responded to a critical argument this way:

---

[57] The original copyright application is available in the Joseph Smith Papers, here: http://www.josephsmithpapers.org/paper-summary/copyright-for-book-of-mormon-11-june-1829/1.

[58] The original printed title page is available in the Joseph Smith Papers, along with helpful historical information, at http://www.josephsmithpapers.org/paper-summary/title-page-of-book-of-mormon-circa-early-june-1829/1#historical-intro.

> The Tanners' assumption that the title page was written as a description of the contents of the Book of Mormon as Joseph Smith conceived it in June 1829 is unwarranted. It was clearly intended to describe Mormon's abridgment only, and not the small plates which became an addendum to his work. Consequently, the abridgment "taken from the plates of Nephi" refers not to the intended replacement for the 116 pages, but to Mormon's work in general.[59]

While I agree that the Tanners' assumption is unwarranted, I don't think Brother Tvedtnes' explanation is an effective response. "Clearly intended" is not a valid argument because the Title Page nowhere evinces an intention to exclude the plates of Nephi from the description of the contents of the book. Saying we know Mormon didn't intend to mention the small plates because the Title Page doesn't mention them is circular reasoning.

So the Tanners have a point. If the small plates were an addendum to the plates Moroni deposited in the stone box, as is commonly assumed, that doesn't explain why the Title Page, which was on the *last leaf* of the plates, would not mention them.

But if, as I propose, the small plates were not part of the collection of plates Joseph originally received from Moroni, then the Title Page makes sense. It was the title page for the *original* Book of Mormon, not for the one we have now (that includes the unabridged small plates).

Even before the Book of Mormon was published, critics noticed this problem with the title page. On February 20, 1830, the *New York Telescope* reprinted comments from C. C. Blatchly, the editor of the *Palmyra Freeman*. After quoting the title page in its entirety, he writes,

---

[59] John A. Tvedtnes, "Book Review of Jerald and Sandra Tanner's Covering Up the Black Hole in the Book of Mormon," in *Review of Books on the Book of Mormon*, Vol. 3 1991, pp. 201-203

> Thus we are informed that this book of Mormon was written (i. e. engraved) by the hand of Mormon, on plates taken from the plates of Nephi; -- **wherefore it is (not a transcript, but what a strange conclusion) an abridgement of the record of Nephi, &c.** If so, why is it not called the record of Nephi?[60] (emphasis added)

One supposes Blatchly would have had more complaints had he known the published text would also contain the *original* writings of Nephi (the small plates) that were not even mentioned in the Title Page.

5. How much Harris wrote. An enigmatic statement by Martin Harris suggests there were two separate translations. Simon Smith interviewed Martin Harris in Clarkston, Utah, in July 1875.[61] According to Smith, Martin said, "I also wrote for him **about one third of the first part of the translation of the plates** as he interpreted them by the Urim and Thummim." (emphasis added)

What did Martin mean?

One could infer that "the first part of the translation" referred to the 116 pages of the Book of Lehi. If so, Martin wrote only 1/3 of the 116 pages, or about 39 pages. That seems unlikely given that he and Joseph worked on the translation continuously from April 12 through June 14.

Nevertheless, some historians have proposed that Emma and her brother may have written 2/3 of the 116 pages.[62] I find

---

[60] Available online at http://www.sidneyrigdon.com/dbroadhu/NY/telescp1.htm#022030.
[61] Smith sent his account of the interview, dated April 30, 1884, to the editor of the *Saints' Herald*, which published it on May 24, 1884. *Opening the Heavens*, p. 136.
[62] Michael Hubbard MacKay and Gerrit J. Dirkmaat, "Firsthand Witness Accounts of the Translation Process," in *The Coming Forth of the Book of Mormon*, (RSC and Deseret Book, 2015) p. 64 and fn11, pp. 74-5.

that unpersuasive, and it's an important enough issue for me to explain why.

These historians cite the Simon Smith account and Emma's 1879 statement that she "frequently wrote day after day." Note that Emma did not specify when, where, or what she wrote on these occasions. She could have been thinking of scribal work for the 116 pages, for the Book of Mosiah, or for 2 Nephi (in Fayette), or any combination of these.

It is very unlikely that Emma would have written twice as much of the manuscript as Martin Harris without anyone remarking on such a considerable contribution, especially when Joseph never gave her that much credit. In 1845, Lucy Mack Smith stated that "Emma had so much of her time taken up with her work that she could not write but little for him,"[63] which is why he prayed for a scribe, a prayer answered by the arrival of Oliver Cowdery.

(This may seem to contradict the idea that Emma scribed most or all of the Book of Mosiah, but considering it took Joseph five months to translate that book before Oliver arrived, the slow pace is consistent with Lucy saying Emma "could not write but little" during this period.)

The historians recognize that Joseph's 1839 history says Martin wrote the 116 pages, but they claim "there is some doubt about [the 1839 history] since he [Joseph] edited the text to read 'we continued, until the 14th of June; having written **216**—pages of manuscript, on foolscap paper.' JSP, H1:244-45."[64] (emphasis added)

The "216 pages" error is in draft 3 of History, circa 1841, in which Howard Coray used numerals instead of spelling out the

---

[63] Lucy Mack Smith (1845), document 106 in *Opening the Heavens*.
[64] https://www.josephsmithpapers.org/paper-summary/history-circa-1841-draft-draft-3/13

Whatever Happened to the Golden Plates?

words.[65] The Coray version is an outlier; "Coray's history work is an artifact demonstrating a course JS considered following for his history but then abandoned."[66]

The version of Joseph's history that appears in the "History of Joseph Smith," published in the *Times and Seasons* on 16 May 1842, says Martin "had written one hundred and sixteen pages of manuscript on foolscap paper."

Another interviewer reported that Martin "said he had written One Hundred and Sixteen pages Foolscap of the translation he said at this period of the Translation a circumstance happened that he was the cause of the One Hundred and Sixteen pages that he had written being lost, and never was found."[67]

Compared with the ambiguous Simon Smith interview, these accounts seem conclusive. Joseph Smith and Martin Harris both say Martin wrote the 116 pages between April 12 and June 14, and no other accounts contradict their statements. There is no record that Emma or Harris ever corrected the *Times and Seasons* account, although they lived for decades after 1842.

Questions remain. If Martin wrote the entire 116 pages, what did Emma write before Martin arrived in 1828? And what did she write before Oliver arrived in 1829?

We simply don't have enough information to know for sure, but there is evidence that Emma wrote some or all of the Book of Mosiah and some portion of 2 Nephi.

Joseph's first interaction with the plates involved copying characters and translating them. Joseph's father claimed there was an alphabet of the unknown language on the plates. Perhaps this experimental material may have been included in what

---

[65] You can see the original manuscript here: http://www.josephsmithpapers.org/paper-summary/history-circa-1841-draft-draft-3/13.

[66] See http://www.josephsmithpapers.org/intro/introduction-to-history-drafts-1838-1842?p=1.

[67] William Pilkington, Affidavit, April 3, 1934, Church Archives; cited in Vogel, *Early Mormon Documents*, 2:353-56, and Welch, *Opening the Heavens*, 140.

Martin took to New York City. Emma could have been involved with this process.

Considering all the evidence, I think it's fair to say we are confident that Martin Harris wrote all, or substantially all, of the 116 pages.[68]

What did Martin mean that he wrote about 1/3 of the "first part of the translation?"

If there is a "first part" of the translation, there is also at least a *second* part. I propose Harris was referring to the translation activity at Harmony as the "first" part, with the second part taking place at Fayette.

Because it is almost certain that Joseph translated the Title Page in Harmony—the "very last leaf" of the collection of plates—it would make sense for Martin to consider the Harmony translation the "first part" of the overall translation. He came to Fayette during the translation of the "second part" so he would know the difference.

This would mean that the 116 pages were about 1/3 of the Harmony translation; i.e., that the balance of the translation, from Mosiah through Moroni, would have to be around 232 pages of equivalent word density.

How would Martin know that?

One way would be if Joseph told him, based on the number of plates translated, that they were 1/3 of the way through the Harmony plates (not counting the sealed portion) when they finished the 116 pages. We have no record of that, however.

But there is a way we could infer this from the Original Manuscript.

Like the Original and Printer's Manuscripts, the 116 pages were written on foolscap paper (large sheets of paper 12-13.5 inches wide and 15-17 inches long).

---

[68] For more information, see the detailed analysis in Don Bradley, *The Lost 116 Pages: Reconstructing the Book of Mormon's Missing Stories* (Greg Kofford Books, Inc., Salt Lake City, UT, 2019).

Whatever Happened to the Golden Plates?

Each sheet was folded in half, either lengthwise or widthwise. This meant each sheet would have four writing surfaces: front and back on both sides of the fold. Normally six sheets of paper would be "gathered" together and bound with string, making 24 pages for each gathering.

We assume the 116 pages were also written on four gatherings of 24 pages each (96 pages), plus one gathering of 20 pages. It is unknown why the final gathering had only 5 sheets, but it seems likely they ran out of the particular type of paper they were using. Royal Skousen, who has studied the Original and Printer's manuscript in considerable depth, notes "In the printer's manuscript, no gathering involves sheets of differing paper. The same appears to hold for the original manuscript."[69] The completion of these gatherings could have made a good reason for Martin to propose taking the manuscript, but there are other possibilities.

At any rate, the 116 pages is an oft-cited number and it fits the normal gathering process, assuming one gathering of 20 pages.

As previously mentioned, most of the Original Manuscript was destroyed by water after Joseph placed it in the cornerstone of the Nauvoo House in Nauvoo. However, about 28% of it survived, including some complete pages.

The principal scribe, Oliver Cowdery, wrote page numbers, but "Unfortunately, there are no extant page numbers in the original manuscript for the translation of the plates of Mormon and Moroni (from the lost book of Lehi through the book of Moroni)."[70]

The last fragment of the text is from Ether 15:17. Skousen estimates that this would be on page 472 if we had the page numbers. This would extrapolate to about 484 pages to the end of Moroni, including the original 116 pages.

---

[69] Royal Skousen, Editor, *The Original Manuscript of the Book of Mormon* (FARMS, BYU, 2001), p. 38.
[70] Ibid, p. 33.

The translation of the plates of Nephi, including the Words of Mormon, took up an estimated 124 pages, for a total of 604 pages of text (484 + 124 - 4 blank leafs). This is an educated guess, because we only have fragments from 236 of the pages.

There are several other complicating factors. The Original Manuscript was written on at least five different paper types. The Fayette translation was written on three types not found in the Harmony translation and the Harmony translation used at least two paper types. The Fayette paper was about one centimeter wider than the Harmony paper. Some of the pages are folded lengthwise while others are widthwise. Different scribes wrote more or less compactly, and even the same scribe was not consistent throughout. We don't have samples of Martin Harris' handwriting to evaluate how compactly he may have written the 116 pages.

Despite the uncertainties, I propose a method for assessing Martin's statement that the 116 pages were about 1/3 of the "first part" of the translation.

First, we should note that the translation of the plates of Nephi (1 Nephi through Words of Mormon) comprises about 24% of the entire text as we have it now—not one-third. Mormon referred to the small plates of Nephi as a "small account" (WoM 1:3). He had already abridged the Book of Lehi when he found this "small account," so we would expect the term "small account" to mean it was shorter than his abridgment of the Book of Lehi. The small account is 24%, substantially less than one third. So far, so good.

Second, if the "first part" of the translation consisted of the Book of Lehi (116 pages), plus Mosiah through Moroni, then the latter section would need to be about 232 pages of equivalent word count. As I mentioned above, Skousen estimates there were about 604 pages in the Original Manuscript. 116 is not close to one-third of 604.

However, there is considerable variation in the Original Manuscript. Page 3, the first page we have because the first two pages were lost or damaged, contains 773 words (1 Ne. 2:2-23).

Whatever Happened to the Golden Plates?

Page 4 contains only 608. The difference is Oliver Cowdery wrote page 3, but John Whitmer started writing part way down on page 4, and his handwriting is much less dense than Oliver's.

Of course, we don't know for sure how many words per page Martin Harris wrote on the 116 pages, but he probably would have tended to write densely to save paper. For this analysis, I assumed Martin would have written like Oliver did on page 3.

To avoid the problems of different folds and different scribes, I compared the first page of the original manuscript with the corresponding text on the printer's manuscript.[71] The printer's manuscript uses a consistent fold and is written almost entirely by Oliver, so it is relatively uniform.

It works out that page 3 of the Original Manuscript contains about as much text as 1.5 pages of the printer's manuscript's version of the same text because of different page sizes and handwriting styles.

If Martin Harris wrote about 775 words/page, there would be around 90,000 words in the 116 pages. The word count of Mosiah through Moroni is around 200,000 words, which makes Martin's contribution about 1/3 of the "first part" of the translation.

I realize these assumptions can be questioned, and I'm not claiming they are necessarily correct, but they do give a rough approximation that supports what Martin said.

By inference, then, the "second part" of the translation took place at Fayette. That would be the translation of the plates of Nephi (1 Nephi through Words of Mormon).

The distinction between the first and second parts of the translation could be based purely on location, but it is also consistent with a distinction between *sets* of plates that were translated. I think the "first part" of the translation was the plates of Mormon and Moroni, accomplished in Harmony, while the "second part" of the translation involved a second set

---

[71] See Appendix 6 for the detailed calculation.

of plates; i.e., the plates of Nephi which Joseph did not have in Harmony.

6. D&C 10 and the plates of Nephi. D&C 10 instructs Joseph not to retranslate the Book of Lehi because of the plans of the wicked men who had taken the 116 pages. Instead, he was instructed to translate the "plates of Nephi." I think this means *he didn't have the plates of Nephi* in Harmony but would get them later when he arrived in Fayette. (We refer to these now as the "small plates of Nephi," but D&C 10 did not refer to them that way.)

The dating of D&C 10 is uncertain. It is probably a compilation of more than one revelation. At one point, it was dated "summer 1828," as the heading in my 1981 printed edition reads. As of December 2016, the digital version of the introduction says it was received "likely around April 1829, though portions may have been received as early as the summer of 1828."[72]

I think Joseph sought and received the revelation in May 1829, at least the portions that refer to the plates of Nephi (starting with verse 38).

Richard Bushman explained the issue this way:

> The order of translation in turn bears on the date of section 10, currently dated "summer 1828"in modern editions of the Doctrine and Covenants. The manuscript version of the History of the Church gives May 1829 for the date of section 10. The Book of Commandments, the first printed version of the Doctrine and Covenants, also dated the section May 1829. A later editor, however, changed the date to summer 1828, because the directions for translating 1 Nephi are in that section. The revelation would have lost its point by May 1829, if Joseph had begun the translation of 1 Nephi long before. On the other hand,

---

[72] The Source Note in the Joseph Smith Papers is similar. https://www.josephsmithpapers.org/paper-summary/revelation-spring-1829-dc-10/1#source-note

if Joseph had not translated 1 Nephi by May because he had started with Mosiah when he resumed work after the loss of the 116 pages, section 10 was relevant in May.

In conjunction with the dating change of section 10, the text of the manuscript was also altered. Insertions and interpositions in the manuscript in another hand changed the words so as to fit section 10 into the chronology where the later editor believed it rightfully belonged. With the information provided in Dean Jessee's analysis, confidence is restored in the original manuscript and dating.[73]

The Historical Introduction to D&C 10 in the Joseph Smith Papers supports this conclusion, but makes the additional observation that May 1829 is a more likely date.

> As JS and Cowdery approached what would become the end of the Book of Mormon, they grew concerned about whether to go back and retranslate the lost portion…. a series of close textual parallels between the featured text and Christ's teachings in the Book of Mormon also support a spring 1829 date. These texts share lengthy phrases, including some not found in the Bible, and suggest a relationship between this revelation and the third book of Nephi in the Book of Mormon, likely dictated in May 1829.[74]

The May 1829 date is consistent with Joseph receiving this revelation about the time when he and Oliver reached the end of the unsealed plates (Moroni 10) and had to decide whether to go back to the beginning and re-translate the Book of Lehi.

As I discussed in a previous section, there is no place in Mormon's abridgement for the record of Nephi. I think D&C 9

---

[73] Richard Lyman Bushman, *Joseph Smith: Rough Stone Rolling*, (Alfred A. Knopf, New York, 2005), note 63 on page 579.
[74] Historical Introduction, *Revelation*, Spring 1829 [D&C 10], online at http://www.josephsmithpapers.org/paper-summary/revelation-spring-1829-dc-10/1.

and 10 explain that the two sets of records were completely separate.

First, let's look at D&C 9:1-2.

> 1 Behold, I say unto you, my son, that because you did not translate according to that which you desired of me, and did commence again to write for my servant, Joseph Smith, Jun., even so I would that ye should continue until you have finished this record, which I have entrusted unto him.
> 2 And then, behold, **other records have I**, that I will give unto you power that you may assist to translate.

This revelation, dated April 1829, is generally understood to refer to a promise that was never fulfilled; i.e., the Lord's assurance that he has other records that he would give Oliver power that he may assist to translate.[75]

But notice the sequence.

First, the Lord asks Oliver to "continue until you have finished *this record*." The reference can be only to the record they were translating in April 1829; i.e., the plates of Mormon and Moroni from the stone box, meaning the abridged plates capped by the Title Page.

Second, the Lord promised that once they finished *this* record, he had *other records* that Oliver could assist to translate.

In the very next section, now D&C 10, the Lord identified these "other records" as the plates of Nephi and then provided them as promised.

After revisiting the loss of the 116 pages and the problem that would result from Joseph re-translating the Book of Lehi, in Section 10 the Lord tells Joseph about *another* set of plates.

---

[75] Some think this passage refers to the Book of Moses and/or the Book of Abraham. While that's possible, the context of the revelation, coming just before D&C 10 when another record is revealed, makes more sense. Separately, I think it's possible at least the first part of the Book of Moses came from plates in the Nephite repository because of Ether 1:4.

38 And now, verily I say unto you, that an account of those things that you have written, which have gone out of your hands, **is engraven upon the plates of Nephi**;
39 Yea, and you remember it was said in those writings that a more particular account was given of these things **upon the plates of Nephi.**
40 And now, because the account which is **engraven upon the plates of Nephi** is more particular concerning the things which, in my wisdom, I would bring to the knowledge of the people **in this account**—
41 Therefore**, you shall translate the engravings which are on the plates of Nephi, down even till you come to the reign of king Benjamin, or until you come to that which you have translated, which you have retained;**
42 And behold, you shall publish it as the **record of Nephi**; and thus I will confound those who have altered my words.
43 I will not suffer that they shall destroy my work; yea, I will show unto them that my wisdom is greater than the cunning of the devil.
44 Behold, they have only got a part, or an abridgment of the **account of Nephi**.
45 Behold, there are many things **engraven upon the plates of Nephi** which do throw greater views upon my gospel; therefore, it is wisdom in me that **you should translate this first part of the engravings of Nephi,** and send forth in this work.

These verses make a sharp distinction between the account on the plates of Nephi and the things contained in "this account," meaning the abridged plates Joseph and Oliver were working with during May 1829.

In fact, the Lord specifies that Joseph was to translate only the "first part" of the engravings of Nephi (verse 45), down to "the reign of king Benjamin" (verse 41), and send them forth "in *this* work," meaning the translation of the plates he possessed in Harmony.

In my view, the plates of Nephi are the "other records" the Lord referred to in D&C 9, for which he promised to give Oliver Cowdery power to assist to translate. This was in *addition* to the translation work Oliver and Joseph were performing in Harmony.

Once they arrived in Fayette, Oliver *did* assist Joseph to translate the other records; i.e., the plates of Nephi.

The promises in D&C 9 were fulfilled to the letter.

Recap:

1. Joseph obtained a set of abridged plates from Moroni's stone box.

2. He took them to Harmony to translate.

3. As Joseph's scribe, Martin Harris wrote about 1/3 of the translation of the unsealed portion of these plates, which totaled 116 pages that were lost. The 116 pages consisted of the Book of Lehi and the first two chapters of the Book of Mosiah. The balance of the translation, Mosiah through Moroni, would have about twice as many words as the 116 pages, so Harris was correct about the 1/3 of the "first part" that he wrote.

4. Oliver Cowdery arrived in April 1829 and acted as Joseph's scribe to complete the translation of the plates from the Book of Mosiah through Moroni.

5. In April, the Lord promised to give Oliver power to assist in translating other records (D&C 9).

6. In May, near the completion of the translation of the plates he possessed, Joseph asked whether to retranslate the Book of Lehi. The Lord told him not to because he needed to translate the plates of Nephi instead—plates Joseph didn't have yet (D&C 10). The plates of Nephi were the "other records" the Lord told Oliver about in D&C 9.

7. The Lord commanded Joseph through the Urim and Thummim to move to Fayette to complete the translation. In Fayette, they translated the plates of Nephi—the "other records" promised in D&C 9.

Conclusion: The plates Moroni put in the stone and cement box on the Hill Cumorah consisted of his father's abridgement of the plates of Nephi, his own abridgement of the book of Ether along with the sealed portion he mentioned, and his own writing as he sealed the record.

That's it.

The original plates of Nephi were not in the box.

Joseph did not obtain them until the divine messenger gave them to him after he arrived in Fayette.

9b The use of the plates.

From the earliest days of the Restoration there have been dual narratives about the translation. Some, including Joseph and Oliver, said that Joseph translated the plates with the Nephite interpreters that accompanied the plates, which they called the Urim and Thummim.

Others claimed Joseph dictated words that appeared on a seer stone he had found before obtaining the plates. The earliest known publication to mention the translation was in the *Palmyra Freeman*, dated August 11, 1829. The author, Jonathan Hadley, strongly opposed the "greatest piece of superstition" and published the account that he attributed to "proselytes" and/or Martin Harris.

> It was said that the leaves of the Bible were plates of gold, about eight inches long, six wide, and one eighth of an inch thick, on which were engraved characters or hieroglyphics. By placing the spectacles in a hat, and looking into it, Smith could (he said so, at least) interpret these characters.[76]

This account has Joseph placing "spectacles" in a hat, referring not to any seer stone but to the Nephite interpreters (the "Urim and Thummim") which Joseph described as "spectacles" in his 1832 history.[77] Yet the same article explained

---

[76] "Golden Bible," *Palmyra Freeman,* Aug. 11, 1829, http://www.olivercowdery.com/smithhome/Phelps/1829_0811PF-pg2.gif See also http://www.ldshistoricalnarratives.com/2023/08/the-jonathan-hadley-account-and-sith.html

[77] "the Lord had prepared spectacles for to read the Book." https://www.josephsmithpapers.org/paper-summary/history-circa-summer-1832/5

that Joseph was prohibited from displaying the interpreters,[78] so the newspaper account reflects confusion about exactly what happened, likely a product of hearsay and/or inferences—if not the author's explicit antagonism toward what he called the "whole Mormon gang."

As we'll discuss in the next section, the various accounts can be reconciled by careful analysis of the evidence. We must distinguish between what people actually saw and what they assumed, or inferred, they saw.

The bottom line: Joseph translated the plates with the Urim and Thummim, but he also used the seer stone as discussed below.

———

Neither Joseph Smith nor Oliver Cowdery described the translation process in as much detail as we would have liked, but they did consistently affirm that Joseph translated the record by means of the Urim and Thummim, or Nephite interpreters, that came with the plates, just as Moroni had instructed him.[79]

Joseph and Oliver were fully aware of the SITH rumors. They dispelled the rumors several times. For example, in 1838, Joseph answered a direct question on the subject.

> Question 4th. How, and where did you obtain the book of Mormon?

---

[78] "He told me... I should not show them to any person; neither the breastplate with the Urim and Thummim; only to those to whom I should be commanded to show them; if I did I should be destroyed." (Joseph Smith—History 1:42)

[79] Moroni said it was Joseph's "privilege, if obedient to the commandments of the Lord, to obtain and translate the same by the means of the Urim and Thummim, which were deposited for that purpose with the record." https://www.josephsmithpapers.org/paper-summary/history-1834-1836/69

Answer. Moroni, the person who deposited the plates, from whence the book of Mormon was translated, in a hill in Manchester, Ontario County New York, being dead; and raised again therefrom, appeared unto me, and told me where they were; and gave me directions how to obtain them. I obtained them, **and the Urim and Thummim with them; by the means of which,** I translated the plates; and thus came the book of Mormon.[80] (emphasis added)

Later, in 1842, Joseph reiterated his claim that he translated the record with the interpreters that came with the plates.

With the records was found a curious instrument which the ancients called "Urim and Thummim," which consisted of two transparent stones set in the rim of a bow fastened to a breastplate. **Through the medium of the Urim and Thummim** I translated the record by the gift, and power of God.[81] (emphasis added)

When Oliver Cowdery rejoined the Church in 1848, he addressed three rumors that were still circulating, including SITH.

I wrote with my own pen the entire Book of Mormon (save a few pages) as it fell from the lips of the Prophet as he translated it by the gift and power of God by means of the Urim and Thummim, or as it is called by that book, holy interpreters. I beheld with my eyes and handled with my hands the gold plates from which it was translated. I also beheld the Interpreters. That book is true. Sidney Rigdon

---

[80] https://www.josephsmithpapers.org/paper-summary/elders-journal-july-1838/10
[81] https://www.josephsmithpapers.org/paper-summary/times-and-seasons-1-march-1842/5

did not write it. Mr. Spaulding did not write it. I wrote it myself as it fell from the lips of the Prophet.[82]

When we realize that Joseph had given Oliver his "seer stone" and that Oliver still possessed the stone on this occasion, his statement is all the more significant. He did not hold up or display the stone when he spoke. He did not use the stone to bolster or corroborate his testimony. Instead, he reaffirmed what he and Joseph had said all along; i.e., that Joseph used the interpreters that came with the plates.

In fact, neither Joseph nor Oliver ever said or implied that Joseph used the seer stone he found in a well (the SITH narrative).

Consequently, whatever the SITH witnesses observed, it could not have been the translation.

———

The inconsistent and even contradictory statements from people who claimed to be eyewitnesses, to the extent they are reliable and credible, can tell us nothing about what was happening in Joseph's mind. In my book *A Man that Can Translate: Joseph Smith and the Nephite Interpreters*, I reconciled the historical evidence by proposing that Joseph actually translated the plates into his own language using the Nephite interpreters—just as he claimed all along.

However, because he was under the commandment to never display the plates or Urim and Thummim, he used SITH to demonstrate or explain the translation process and to "satisfy the awful curiosity" of his supporters and family.

Joseph was explicit about the translation when he explained how he learned the Nephite language.

———

[82] https://www.lettervii.com/p/oliver-returning-to-church-reuben.html

I [was] enabled to reach the place of my destination in Pennsylvania; and immediately after my arrival there **I commenced copying the characters off the plates. I copied a considerable number of them, and by means of the Urim and Thummim I translated some of them**, which I did between the time I arrived at the house of my wife's father, in the month of December, and the February following.[83]

From this passage, we see Joseph learning the Nephite language by studying the characters for several months prior to dictating a translation to Martin Harris (the 116 pages). To be sure, we can't say for sure how Joseph translated "by means of the Urim and Thummim," but the Lord explained to the brother of Jared,

> 23 And behold, these two stones will I give unto thee, and ye shall seal them up also with the things which ye shall write.
> 24 For behold, the language which ye shall write I have confounded; wherefore I will cause in my own due time that these stones shall **magnify to the eyes of men** these things which ye shall write. (Ether 3:23–24)

We infer that "magnify" in this passage refers to a spiritual magnification—an example of a "gift of tongues" interpretation—but it could also refer to a physical magnification. Perhaps one reason why Joseph copied the characters was to enlarge them and make them more legible.

Regardless of how the Urim and Thummim functioned, as we saw above, Joseph and Oliver emphasized that this was the instrument he used.

---

[83] Joseph Smith – History 1:62, online at https://www.churchofjesuschrist.org/study/scriptures/pgp/js-h/1?lang=eng.

Joseph's mother, Lucy Mack Smith, reported another usage in Harmony, near the end of the translation of the abridged plates, when she referred to

> an intimation that was given **through the urim and thumim** for as he one morning **applied them to his eyes to look upon the record** instead of the words of the book being given him he was commanded to write a letter to one David Whitmer this man Joseph had never seen but he was instructed to say him that he must come with his team immediately in order to convey Joseph and his family Oliver [Cowdery] back to his house which was 135 miles that they might remain with him there untill the translation should be completed for that an evil designing people were seeking to take away Joseph's life in order to prevent the work of God from going forth among the world.[84]

But, as indicated in the 1829 *Palmyra Freeman*, some people thought Joseph translated by looking at a stone (or spectacles) in a hat.

The 1834 anti-Mormon book *Mormonism Unvailed* described SITH as an alternative to the Urim and Thummim:

> The plates, therefore, which had been so much talked of, were found to be of no manner of use. After all, the Lord showed and communicated to him every word and letter of the Book. **Instead of looking at the characters inscribed upon the plates, the prophet was obliged to resort to the old "peep stone,"** which he formerly used in money - digging. **This he placed in a hat**, or box, into which he also thrust his face….
> **Another account** they give of the transaction, is, that it was performed with **the big spectacles** before mentioned, and which were in fact, the identical **Urim and Thumim**

---

[84] https://www.josephsmithpapers.org/paper-summary/lucy-mack-smith-history-1844-1845/100

mentioned in Exodus 28...[85] (emphasis added)

Oliver Cowdery responded to these false claims by affirming that Joseph used the Urim and Thummim--not the one mentioned in Exodus, but the Nephite interpreters.

> These were days never to be forgotten—to sit under the sound of a voice dictated by the inspiration of heaven, awakened the utmost gratitude of this bosom! Day after day I continued, uninterrupted, to write from his mouth, as **he translated with the Urim and Thummim, or, as the Nephites would have said, 'Interpreters,'** the history or record called 'The Book of Mormon.'
> (Joseph Smith—History, Note, 1) (emphasis added)

Recall Joseph's statement that "it was not intended to tell the world all the particulars of the coming forth of the book of Mormon." One view, suggested by Dr. Francis Kirkham, is that "it may not have been expedient for the Prophet to try and explain the method of translation for the reason his hearers would lack the capacity to understand. It seemed sufficient to them at that time to know that the translation had been made by the gift and power of God."

Another explanation is the one suggested by Brigham Young, who, when describing Oliver's visits to the repository in Cumorah/Ramah, said Oliver "did not take the liberty of telling such things in meeting as I take." He told Brigham about the visits privately, knowing that public discussion would only encourage people to go looking for the plates. The less said about them, the better.

Those possibilities, combined with the strict commandment to never display the plates or the interpreters, provide a rationale

---

[85] *Mormonism Unvailed*, p. 18, available online at. https://play.google.com/books/reader?id=KXJNAAAAYAAJ&printsec=frontcover&pg=GBS.PA18

for why Joseph would use SITH to explain and demonstrate the process. But such a demonstration does not mean Joseph did not use the plates to translate.

My proposal that Joseph translated two sets of plates relies on the critical assumption that Joseph did actually use the plates during the translation. Otherwise, it wouldn't matter whether he possessed the plates of Nephi at all. They could have been anywhere on earth. Mormon's greatest fears could have been realized; the Lamanites could have found them and destroyed them. It still wouldn't matter because the seer stone could still have shown Joseph the words he needed to dictate.

Joseph's use of the plates has been the topic of considerable speculation. A 2003 student manual explains:

> Little is known about the actual process of translating the record, primarily because those who knew the most about the translation, Joseph Smith and Oliver Cowdery, said the least about it. Moreover, Martin Harris, David Whitmer, and Emma Smith, who assisted Joseph, left no contemporary descriptions. The sketchy accounts they recorded much later in life were often contradictory.[86]

The "sketchy" accounts by Martin, David and Emma refer in part to the question of whether Joseph translated the engravings or merely read words that appeared on the seer stone, Joseph's use of a hat during the translation process, and how much the translation reflects Joseph's own language.

When interpreting events in Church history, it's a mistake to accept isolated statements at face value, particularly when the witnesses were not cross-examined or confronted with contrary evidence. Unlike secular history, Church history involves revelations and interactions with various divine messengers.

---

[86] *Church History in the Fulness of Times Student Manual* (Salt Lake City: The Church of Jesus Christ of Latter-day Saints, 2003), 58

Faithful analysis requires us to evaluate the historical evidence in light of the revelations.

D&C 10:41, for example, says "you shall translate the engravings which are on the plates of Nephi." This tells us Joseph was translating *engravings*, or characters, on specific plates. If he never consulted the plates, this revelation would be meaningless to him.

No other explanation makes sense in the totality of the circumstances. If Joseph never used the plates to translate, what was the point of having a portion of them sealed? If all he did was read from the stone (or even the interpreters) without referring to the actual plates, the stone would not have presented the forbidden material in the sealed portion anyway.

An argument can be made—I've made it myself in the past—that even if he didn't use the plates to translate, Joseph needed the plates as assurance that he was not being deceived by some evil spirit. The antiquity of the plates gave him a basis for exercising the faith he needed to operate the seer stone. Plus, the plates gave others confidence that Joseph was telling the truth. After all, none of the 11 witnesses ever denied their testimony of having seen the plates.

Alternatively, the plates may have served as a sort of talisman or catalyst, a prompt for him to receive revelation.

Such arguments may have merit as far as they go, but they strain credulity and fall short of accommodating the language of the revelations or the historical evidence that Joseph actually used the plates during the translation.[87]

The many accounts of the translation process contain inconsistencies that cannot be easily reconciled unless we recognize that they are typical of many witness statements; i.e., while the statements may include accurate *observations* made at

---

[87] Several authors have discussed the catalyst idea, pro and con. For example, https://www.fromthedesk.org/richard-bushman-gold-plates/.

various times and places, they are also mingled with the witnesses' subjective assumptions and inferences.

Use of the plates. From the earliest days of the Church through the present, there have been claims that Joseph didn't actually use the plates—i.e., they sat on the table under a cloth, or were hidden out in the woods while he read the words that appeared on the seer stone, putting his face in a hat to block out the ambient light. [88]

There are accounts to that effect, but they contradict what Joseph himself said. Thus, whatever Joseph may have done with the stone in the hat, it was not translating.

Although Joseph said it was "not intended to tell the world all the particulars" of the coming forth of the Book of Mormon, many particulars have been published over the years. People left several accounts describing the translation. Some of these are hearsay, but others are from people who were, or claim to have been, present during the translation itself. These include accounts from Martin Harris, David Whitmer, and Emma Smith.

Many of the accounts refer to Joseph putting the interpreters or the stone into a hat to block out the light so he could read the words that appeared. That has led people to assume he didn't use the plates themselves.

According to this theory, somehow the English words appeared on the interpreters and all Joseph had to do was read them. I don't think that theory can be reconciled with D&C 8-9, specifically, D&C 9:7. "Behold, you have not understood; you have supposed that I would give it unto you, when you took no thought save it was to ask me."

---

[88] For a more detailed discussion, see my books *A Man that Can Translate* and *By Means of the Urim and Thummim*, co-authored with James Lucas.

A good place to start is the Gospel Topics essay titled "Book of Mormon Translation."[89] The essay summarizes several accounts of observers and suggests that Joseph used a variety of techniques. As an introduction to the topic, it is helpful, but it falls short of reaffirming what Joseph and Oliver always taught. Actually, the essay never quotes what Joseph and Oliver taught.

There are several theories about how this process functioned.[90] The range of multiple working hypotheses includes those who say it doesn't matter how Joseph produced the Book of Mormon because it is true regardless. Others say it matters a great deal how the book originated because its truthfulness depends on its origin.

In my view, the material reality of the plates is integral to accepting the authenticity of both Joseph's explanation and the historicity of the text.

One sign of veracity is when an important fact is taken for granted. The existence of two separate sets of plates that Joseph obtained separately and translated in two separate locations not only helps us understand and reconcile the historical accounts, but also reinforces and corroborates the testimonies of the Three and Eight Witnesses.

The essay includes this explanation of the translation process from Oliver Cowdery.

> The principal scribe, Oliver Cowdery, testified under oath in 1831 that Joseph Smith "found with the plates, from which he translated his book, two transparent stones, resembling glass, set in silver bows. That by looking through these, he was able to read

---

[89] The essay is online here:
https://www.churchofjesuschrist.org/study/manual/gospel-topics-essays/book-of-mormon-translation?lang=eng. A detailed analysis is here: https://www.ldshistoricalnarratives.com/2022/09/analysis-gospel-topics-essay-on-book-of.html.
[90] For an analysis of all the theories, see *By Means of the Urim and Thummim*.

Whatever Happened to the Golden Plates?

in English, the reformed Egyptian characters, which were engraven on the plates." In the fall of 1830, Cowdery visited Union Village, Ohio, and spoke about the translation of the Book of Mormon. Soon thereafter, a village resident reported that the translation was accomplished by means of "two transparent stones in the form of spectacles thro which the translator looked on the engraving." [original citations omitted]

As the principal scribe, and the only person we know of (besides Joseph) who was authorized by the Lord to attempt a translation himself, Oliver Cowdery would be in the best position to know how the translation was done. In these accounts, Oliver describes Joseph looking through the interpreters at the engraving, much as Joseph's mother Lucy described Joseph using the Urim and Thummim to look on the plates when he was directed to contact David Whitmer.

It's significant that Lucy was not writing to describe how Joseph translated the plates or how he used the urim and Thummim. She mentioned that in passing only because of the commandment Joseph received to write to David Whitmer. I read this account as saying the equivalent of this: "Of course Joseph looked upon the record with the urim and thumim. He did it every day. Just in this one case, he received an unexpected commandment to contact a man he didn't know."

Instruments used. Some accounts say Joseph used the interpreters (the ones Moroni left in the stone box with the plates). Others say Joseph used a seer stone. Others say he used both. Emma said he used the interpreters until Martin Harris lost the 116 pages, and thereafter used the seer stone.

These accounts are characteristic of eyewitness testimony. People see things (and remember them) through their own filters, and they relate the same events differently under different circumstances, often in response to different questions. Their accounts may be accurate, but can never be complete or comprehensive; a person's *account* of an event is subjective because every sensory experience, every memory and every recitation of that memory is selective and unique to each individual.

In some cases, people may have been influenced by what others said. People conflate others' memories with their own. That's why we consider whether there is anything particularly memorable about an event, such as David Whitmer hearing the word *Cumorah* for the first time, or seeing Joseph turn unusually pale.

I think the best way to resolve these specific discrepancies is to conclude that while Joseph used the interpreters to translate, he used SITH to explain and demonstrate the process.

Why SITH? Although Joseph and Oliver (and the revelations in the Doctrine and Covenants) always say Joseph translated the engravings on the plates by means of the Urim and Thummim, there are many accounts by others that relate the stone-in-the-hat (SITH) scenario.

Some writers have attributed SITH to enemies of Joseph Smith; i.e., they claim the SITH accounts were false accounts designed to discredit Joseph Smith.

That approach can't entirely account for the earliest accounts of the translation, such as the one we saw in the 1829 *Palmyra Freeman* (the spectacles in the hat). The newspaper implied the information came from Martin Harris, who at the time was mortgaging his farm to pay for the printing. He was the opposite of an enemy at that time. If anything, he wanted people to accept the Book of Mormon (and buy a copy). But as we noted previously, the account came from Jonathan Hadley, a harsh critic, and is confused because although no one could have seen the "spectacles" mentioned, they could have observed SITH during the demonstration in Fayette.

If the information came from Martin, who was not present for the translation in Fayette, Martin was relating hearsay; i.e., what others said who had observed the demonstration.

As mentioned in the Gospel Topics Essay, there are several statements made by (or attributed to) David Whitmer, Martin

Harris, and Emma Smith that relate some form of SITH. While it's true that David and Martin left the Church, and Emma had her own issues, in every case, these three people consistently sought to support the divine authenticity of the Book of Mormon.

These statements were made many years and decades after the events. The lateness of the statements doesn't necessarily invalidate them, but it does raise the question of why they thought SITH would promote faith in the divinity of the Book of Mormon.

This question leads us back to the 1834 book *Mormonism Unvailed*. That book proposed that when Joseph dictated from behind the "vail" or curtain, he was actually reading a novel written by Solomon Spalding. The Spalding theory became the predominant explanation for the Book of Mormon among nonbelievers. It was repeated in numerous books and articles.

As we saw, Joseph and Oliver refuted the SITH claims in *Mormonism Unvailed* by reaffirming that Joseph translated the plates with the Nephite interpreters.

They also refuted the Spalding theory by emphasizing the narrative related actual history. As evidence, they cited the fact that the Hill Cumorah of Mormon 6:6 was in western New York.

As we discussed previously, Joseph also explained that the title page "is a literal translation, taken from the very last leaf, on the left-hand side of the collection or book of plates, which contained the record which has been translated, the language of the whole running the same as all Hebrew writing in general." This statement reflects a familiarity with the plates and the language that far exceeds the use of the plates as a mere stage prop.

A version of the translation that has Joseph merely reading words on a stone contradicts everything he and Oliver taught.

———

But the problem remained. If Joseph dictated the text from behind a "vail" and no one saw the plates or interpreters, then how could anyone prove Joseph was not simply reading the Spalding manuscript?

The Spalding theory became such a threat that in their statements, David and Emma both addressed Spalding before relating the SITH account.[91]

In this historical context, SITH became an apologetic defense of the Book of Mormon. David, Martin and Emma could legitimately and truthfully testify about observing SITH, even if that was only a demonstration. But at least they could emphasize (as they did) that Joseph had nothing to read from, no manuscript or book, etc.

It was the perfect defense against the Spalding theory.

And yet, none of Joseph's contemporaries or successors in Church leadership promoted SITH. They always reiterated the claim from Joseph and Oliver that Joseph translated the engravings on the plates by means of the Nephite interpreters.

In recent years, many critical scholars have revived the SITH claims from *Mormonism Unvailed* and the apologetic SITH statements by David, Martin and Emma. Even some faithful scholars have embraced SITH. Accepting these statements at face value, some people have alleged that Joseph and Oliver misled everyone by claiming Joseph used the Urim and Thummim.

In my view, the evidence of the existence of two separate sets of plates corroborates the testimonies of Joseph and Oliver that Joseph did, indeed, translate actual plates. The Lord directed Joseph to translate the plates of Nephi because without those actual plates, he could not have produced the translation.

While the SITH accounts are understandable from a 19th century apologetic framework, the Spalding theory was

---

[91] For a detailed discussion, see *A Man that Can Translate*.

debunked in the late 1900s. SITH may have served a purpose in its day, but it is no longer viable.

Gallons of ink (and billions of electrons) have been spilled over the question of the translation. I think the evidence shows that Joseph actually translated the engravings on the plates, that it mattered which plates he had, and that he accomplished the translation using his own vocabulary and by means of the Urim and Thummim, meaning the Nephite interpreters Moroni provided.

Elder George A. Smith addressed this specific issue. "When the Lord reveals anything to men He reveals it in language that accords with their own. If any of you were to converse with an angel, and you used strictly grammatical language he would do the same. But if you used two negatives in a sentence the heavenly messenger would use language to correspond with your understanding, and this very objection to the Book of Mormon is an evidence in its favor."[92]

Before concluding this chapter, I'd like to mention an important statement from Oliver Cowdery. Notice that here, his final recorded statement about the translation, he felt the need to specifically refute the Spalding theory.

When Oliver returned to the Church in 1848, Reuben Miller recorded his statement that "I wrote with my own pen the entire Book of Mormon (save a few pages) as it fell from the lips of the prophet. As he translated it by the gift and power of God. By means of the urum [sic] and thummum [sic], or as it is called by that book holy Interpreters. I beheld with my eyes. And handled with my hands the gold plates from which it was translated. I also beheld the Interpreters. That book is true.

---

[92] George A. Smith, "The Sacrament," *Journal of Discourses* 12:335 (15 November 1868), online at http://jod.mrm.org/12/332.

Sidney Rigdon did not write it. Mr Spaulding did not write it. I wrote it myself as it fell from the lips of the prophet."[93]

Although I wasn't present at the translation, I fully accept Oliver Cowdery's statement here. Joseph did translate the plates. It was not a form of spirit writing.

And he could only have done so by the gift and power of God.

---

[93] *Reuben Miller Journal*, October 21, 1848, available online at the Church History Library, MS 1392/f0001/v0001_00015.jpg.
https://dcms.lds.org/delivery/DeliveryManagerServlet?dps_pid=IE1899363 and https://catalog.churchofjesuschrist.org/record/0448e354-d892-4ea7-9e2a-28b714114909/22222322-f4fe-41e3-aa86-bfc54b94df92?view=browse&subView=arrangement

10 The Witnesses

The Three Witnesses signed the statement that has been published with the text from the first edition in 1830. We don't have the original copy with their signatures, but they independently verified that they did sign the statement and they affirmed its contents throughout their lives.

Over the years, the Three Witnesses provided a variety of descriptions of the event. As early as 1831 the *Reflector*, a Palmyra newspaper critical of the Mormons, observed, "There appears to be a great discrepancy, in the stories told by the famous three witnesses to the Gold Bible; and these pious reprobates, individually, frequently give different versions of the same transaction."[94]

Sometimes it seems that they were describing two different experiences—and in my view they were. The accounts make sense when viewed through the later experiences these men had with the repository of Nephite records in the Hill Cumorah.

"The Experience of the Three Witnesses"[95] points out that Oliver, David and Martin desired to be the witnesses. Joseph consulted the Urim and Thummim and obtained a revelation for them (D&C 17):

> 1 Behold, I say unto you, that you must rely upon my word, which if you do with full purpose of heart, you shall have a **view of the plates, and also of the breastplate, the sword of Laban, the Urim and Thummim**, which were given to the brother of Jared upon the mount, when he talked with the Lord face to face, **and**

---

[94] This source is discussed later in this chapter.
[95] Larry E. Morris, "The Experience of the Three Witnesses," *Revelations in Context*, online at
https://www.churchofjesuschrist.org/study/manual/revelations-in-context/the-experience-of-the-three-witnesses?lang=eng .

the miraculous directors which were given to Lehi while in the wilderness, on the borders of the Red Sea.
2 And it is by your faith that you shall obtain a view of them, even by that faith which was had by the prophets of old.
3 And after that you have obtained faith, and have seen them with your eyes, **you shall testify of them**, by the power of God…

Although the revelation is dated June 1829, the earliest version we have is from Revelation Book 2, copied not before 25 Nov. 1834. It was not included in the Book of Commandments. The Source Note in the Joseph Smith papers point out that "Some language used in the version copied into Revelation Book 2 does not fit an 1829 context, suggesting that version was modified from the original, although the degree of modification cannot be known."[96] The part referring to the sword of Laban and the other artifacts was written and corrected, which could have been due to a copy error or might reflect a revision/addition.

A note to verse 2 (above) explains, "For the most part, Cowdery, Harris, and Whitmer focused on the plates in their public testimonies. Whitmer did, however, make repeated reference to seeing the other objects as well."

The first obvious question is why D&C 17 refers to the other artifacts, and requires the witnesses to testify of "them," yet the official testimony of the Three Witnesses refers only to the plates. If they saw all these objects in late June 1829, why didn't the Three Witnesses mention them in their statement?

I have not found a public statement by Oliver or Martin claiming they saw anything other than the plates in June 1829. In the sole contemporaneous account I have found, David also stated merely that the angel showed them the plates.

---

[96] See the Source Note for D&C 17 in the Joseph Smith Papers in *Documents*, Vol. 1, p. 82, available online at http://www.josephsmithpapers.org/paper-summary/revelation-june-1829-e-dc-17/1.

Whatever Happened to the Golden Plates?

After the experience with the Three Witnesses, Joseph returned to the Whitmer house. His mother described the circumstance:

> They returned to the house it was betweeen 3 & 4 o'clock Mrs. [Mary Musselman] Whitmer & Mr. Smith [Joseph Smith Sr.] and myself were sitting in a bedroom I sat on the bed side when Joseph came in he threw himself <down> beside me Father!— Mother!— said he you do not know how happy I am The Lord has **caused the plates to be shown** to 3 more besides me who have also seen an angel and will have to testify to the [truth] of what I have said for they know for themselves that I do not go about to deceive the people and I do feel as though I was relieved of a dreadful burden which was almost too much for me to endure, but they will now have to bear a part and it does rejoice my soul that I am not any longer to be entirely alone in the world. Martin Harris then came in he seemed almost overcome with excess of Joy He then testified to what he had seen and heard as did also the others Oliver and David their testimony was the same <in substance as that> contained in the book of Mormon[97] (emphasis added).

Joseph referred to the angel and the plates, but not to any other artifacts.

It wasn't until fifty years later that David began describing these other artifacts. The Morris article explains that in 1881 David stated that it was in the latter part of June, 1829, when he, Joseph and Oliver were together, and

> the angel showed them [the plates] to us. . . . [We were] sitting on a log when we were overshadowed by a light more glorious than that of the sun. In the midst of this light, but a few feet from us, appeared a table upon which were many golden plates, also the sword of Laban and the directors. I saw them as plain as I see you

---

[97] Lucy Mack Smith, *History*, 1844-1845, p. 11, book 8, online at http://www.josephsmithpapers.org/paper-summary/lucy-mack-smith-history-1844-1845/103.

now, and distinctly heard the voice of the Lord declaring that the records of the plates of the Book of Mormon were translated by the gift and power of God.[98]

David repeated similar statements on other occasions, the first being his statement to Edward Stevenson in 1877.

Why would David wait until 1877 to provide the details of an event that occurred in 1829? And why didn't Martin and Oliver ever mention this publicly?

There is another anomaly. The early accounts by the Three Witnesses say the angel appeared and showed the plates, turning the leaves over. This is consistent with the words of the official testimony:

> And we declare with words of soberness, that an angel of God came down from heaven, and **he brought and laid before our eyes, that we beheld and saw the plates**, and the engravings thereon; and we know that it is by the grace of God the Father, and our Lord Jesus Christ, that we beheld and bear record that these things are true.

But other times they also said they handled the plates. Detractors claim this shows the witnesses had a purely spiritual experience that they had difficulty describing. Supporters claim the witnesses may have handled the plates on another occasion, such as during the translation process when they were covered with a cloth. But Martin Harris said he handled them plate after plate, which he could not feasibly do if they were covered at the time. The witnesses also described the engravings on the plates.

In my view, the best explanation for these inconsistencies is this sequence.

---

[98] *Kansas City Journal*, 5 June 1881, reported in Cook, *David Whitmer Interviews*, p. 63.

Whatever Happened to the Golden Plates?

1. During the translation process, the witnesses may have moved or held the plates while they were concealed under the cloth, as when Martin Harris held them on his knee and when Emma moved them around on the table.

2. None of the witnesses saw the plates uncovered until their experience with the angel in June 1829.

3. The angel showed them the plates and turned them over so the witnesses could see the engravings but did not show them anything else. Hence, the official testimony of the Three Witnesses mentions only the plates.

4. Later, the witnesses saw and hefted the artifacts in the repository in the Hill Cumorah, as reported by Brigham Young and others (see Chapter 12), in fulfillment of the rest of D&C 17. However, the witnesses were forbidden to discuss the repository publicly. It is possible that D&C 17 was reworded to reflect this event, which may explain why we do not have the original copy of the revelation or even the copy that was in Revelation Book 1, and why it was not published in the Book of Commandments.

5. At some point, David Whitmer mentioned the other artifacts, and to avoid discussing the repository, he began telling interviewers that he had seen them during the June 1829 experience in Fayette. In these accounts, he mentioned the table that no other witnesses mentioned, but which matches the accounts of the table in the repository. I view this as his effort to be honest about what he saw without revealing the existence of the repository, possibly because Joseph said, in the October 1831 conference, that it was not intended for that information regarding the "coming forth of the Book of Mormon" to be disclosed.

6. Some or all of the witnesses, along with Joseph's brothers, helped move the plates from the Hill Cumorah to another location for safekeeping.

As you read the following statements, see if you can think of a better explanation.[99]

Martin handled the plates:
1831 – He [Martin] told all about the gold plates, Angels, Spirits, and Jo Smith.—He had **seen and handled them all**, by the power of God! OTH #136, p. 176.
1859 – At one time, Martin said "as many of the plates as Joseph Smith translated **I handled with my hands, plate after plate**." OTH #46, p. 133.
1922 – "I saw the angel, I heard his voice, **I saw and handled the plates** upon which the Book of Mormon was written." OTH #61, p. 139.
1923 – "with these hands," holding out his hands, "**I handled the plates** containing the record of the Book of Mormon." OTH #62, p. 139.

Martin saw the angel handle the plates:
1874 – "The angel **showed me the plates** and I heard the voice of God declare they were translated correctly." OTH #50, p. 135.
1875 - "I do say that the angel **did show to me the plates** containing the Book of Mormon." OTH #51, p. 135.
1918 – "And we did kneel down and pray immediately the angel stood before me and said: "Look' and when I glanced at the angel, I fell but I stood on my feet and **seen the angel turn the leaves of gold** and I said 'It is enough my Lord and my God.'" OTH #60, p. 138.
1925 – "**I saw the plates**." OTH #63, p. 139.
1933 – "And **I saw with these two eyes the angel stand with the gold plates in his hands, and I saw him turn leaf by leaf the plates of gold,** and I also heard the voice of the Lord saying that these words were true and translated correctly." OTH #64, p. 139.
1933 – "I saw the angel and **saw the plates** from which the Book of Mormon was translated." OTH #65, p. 140.

---

[99] References are to *Opening the Heavens* (OTH), *David Whitmer Interviews* (*Interviews*), and *Early Mormon Documents* (EMD).

Whatever Happened to the Golden Plates?

1940 – "After the angel had **shown him the plates** and disappeared, he heard a voice from Heaven that thrilled every fiber of his body." OTH #68, p. 141.

Oliver handled the plates:
1848 – ""I beheld with my eyes. **And handled with my hands the gold plates** from which it was translated." OTH #72, p. 143

Oliver saw the angel handle the plates:
1886 – "He testified that he beheld the plates, the leaves **being turned over by the angel**." OTH #74, p. 143.

David handled the plates:
1882 – We asked him if his testimony was the same now as it was at the time the Book of Mormon was published, regarding seeing the plates and the angel. He rose to his feet, stretched out his hands and said: "**These hands handled the plates**, these eyes saw the angel, and these ears heard his voice." *Interviews*, p. 92.

1885 – He [David] said… that there was nothing between them and the angel except a log that had fallen in the forest… that **he did see and handle the plates**. *Interviews*, p. 163.

1886 – Mr. Whitmer describes every detail of the "vision" with great precision and much fervency, and **insists that he handled and scrutinized the plates,** and that the form and appearance of the strangely engraved characters were so impressed upon his memory that he would never forget them…

David saw the angel handle the plates:
1831 – "Next day [March 28, 1830] we… tarried at the house of Mr. Whitmer…. They affirmed, that **an angel had showed** them certain plates of metal, having the appearance of gold." OTH #131, p. 175.

1876 – "I personally heard him [David] state in Jan. 1876 in his own house…in most positive language, that he did truly see in broad day light, a bright, and most beautiful being, an 'Angel from Heaven,' **who did hold in his hands the golden plates, which he turned over leaf by leaf**, explaining the contents, here and there." EMD 5:26.

1878 – "I saw the angel, and I saw the sword of Laban, and the breast-plate, and the Urim and Thummim, and the plates, and the director, and the angel stood before us, and **he turned the leaves one by one.** I – Did **the angel turn all the leaves before you** as you looked on it? He – No, not all, **only that part of the book which was not sealed**, and what there was sealed appeared as solid to my view as wood." *Interviews*, p. 20.

1881 – "When did you see the plates?" "It was in the latter part of June, 1829. Joseph, Oliver Cowdery and myself were together, and the angel showed them to us. **We not only saw the plates of the book of Mormon**, but he also showed us the brass plates of the book of Ether and many others. They were shown to us in this way. Joseph and Oliver and I were sitting on a log when we were overshadowed by a light more glorious than that of the sun. In the midst of this light, but a few feet from us, appeared a table upon which were many golden plates, also the sword of Laban and the directors." *Interviews*, p. 63.

1883 – "I heard the voice of the angel, **and saw the engravings on the plates, and the plates** just as stated in the Book of Mormon.... You see that small table by the wall? Well, there was a table about that size, and the heavenly messenger brought the several plates and laid them on the table before our eyes, and we saw them, and bore testimony of them, and our testimony is true." *Interviews*, p. 98.

1885 – "Do you know that the plates seen with the Angel (on the table) were real metal, did you touch them? Ans—**We did not touch nor handle the plates**." *Interviews*, p. 152.

1885 – He [David] described to me the details of the occasion, of **the angel presenting the plates** from which the Book of Mormon was translated. The scene was in the woods, with nothing between the angel and himself except a log that had fallen and was lying between them. *Interviews*, p. 160.

My proposal that David intentionally conflated his experiences may seem deceitful on one level, but can also be seen as telling the truth safely. If, as I propose, the existence of the repository was to be kept secret to prevent a reinvigorated treasure hunt once the Book of Mormon was published with the statements of the witnesses about the reality of the plates, David Whitmer was in a bind. Having testified he had seen the items specified in D&C 17, which was copied in Revelation Book 2 but not before 25 Nov. 1834 (and published in the Doctrine and Covenants in 1835), but also forbidden to speak publicly about the repository, the only alternative that made sense was to merge the two experiences. That way, he was telling the truth about what he saw—just not when and where he saw these things.

It is possible David visited the repository soon after the June experience in Fayette anyway; he may have deemed the repository experience as an extension of the visit of the angel with the plates near Fayette.

This would make even more sense if an angel participated in the experience in the repository as well.

Joseph Smith Sr. also told variations of his experiences, based on the circumstances. An 1833 account claims that "The elder Joseph would say that he had seen the plates, and that he knew them to be gold; at other times he would say that they looked like gold; and other times he would say he had not seen the plates at all." OTH #153, p. 181.

The discrepancies in the accounts may be partly due to miscommunication or inaccurate reporting by the listeners, but it makes more sense to me that these witnesses were telling the truth about what they saw and did. They just commingled the experiences to protect the secrecy of the repository of Nephite records.

The official joint declaration includes an interesting change from the Title Page:

> Be it known unto all nations, kindreds, tongues, and people, unto whom this work shall come: That we, through the grace of God the Father, and our Lord Jesus Christ, **have seen the plates which contain this record, which is a record of the people of Nephi**, and also of the Lamanites, their brethren, **and also of the people of Jared**, who came from the tower of which hath been spoken.

There is no mention here of an abridgment. The phrase "a record of the people of Nephi" can include both Mormon's abridgment (the Harmony plates) and the original plates of Nephi (the Fayette plates). This raises the possibility that they knew the finished Book of Mormon contained the original writings of Nephi through Amaleki in addition to the abridgements of the Nephite and Jaredite records as described by the title page.

11 Mormon "put them with"

In Chapter 9a, I discussed why there was no physical place in the abridgement for Mormon to put the original plates of Nephi.

Nevertheless, people have long assumed that Mormon somehow *attached* the small plates of Nephi to his own abridgment; i.e., that he put the three ring binders through his abridgement as well as the small plates. That is the premise for the tradition that Joseph translated only one set of plates.

While this is not an unreasonable interpretation of Words of Mormon, a closer look supports a different view.

The Words of Mormon through verse 11 make sense as a sort of title page for the small plates of Nephi. (Note that ancient people put the Title Page at the end. Joseph explained that the title page was found on the last leaf of the collection of plates.) I propose that Mormon found the small plates, added his commentary, and kept them close by where he could refer to them as he edited the large plates. He did not attach them to his abridgment.

In Words of Mormon 1:1-7, Mormon describes his discovery and inclusion of Nephi's plates. The text is in **bold** below, and I've added my interlinear notes in brackets. I realize this is a lot of detail, but it's important to go through it step-by-step.

Words of Mormon 1:1
1 And now I, Mormon, being about to deliver up the record which I have been making into the hands of my son Moroni,

[Traditionally, this passage has been interpreted to mean Mormon was finished with his abridgment at this point, but I think that's an error. Mormon tells us he is still making the record; "have been making" is continuous, vs. "have made" which would mean the record was completed. This suggests that Mormon was giving his abridgment to his son in stages, as he completed major portions; i.e., the abridgment he has been making up to this point, which was the Book of Lehi. This makes practical sense for several reasons. Maybe Moroni was proofreading it. Maybe Mormon wanted his son to learn the history and ask questions. Maybe Mormon was concerned that he might not be able to finish the entire abridgment, or he gave the plates to Moroni for safekeeping. Regardless of the reason, we see in Mormon 6:6 that even after he finished his own book after abridging the entire Nephite history, he was giving Moroni only "these few plates," suggesting that Moroni already had most of the records. Although the binding method is never mentioned in the text, we know from Joseph Smith and the witnesses that the plates were ultimately bound with three rings. We have no indication that Mormon ever bound the plates. Moroni added his own plates, along with his abridgment of the plates of Ether and the sealed portion. While we can infer Mormon bound his abridgment with the three rings, the text never tells us that. However, Moroni definitely added material to his father's abridgment. It could be Moroni who created the rings and compiled the final set of plates.]

(1 continued) behold I have witnessed almost all the destruction of my people, the Nephites.

[Mormon has witnessed "almost all" the destruction; i.e., they are not yet completely destroyed. As we see in the next verse, he's nowhere near Cumorah at this point. Also, note that to make his record, Mormon had to get the large plates from Ammaron's repository in Jashon (Mormon 2:17), presumably when he was 24 years old, as instructed (Mormon 1:3).]

2 And it is many hundred years

["Many hundred years" is really only about 400 years.]

Whatever Happened to the Golden Plates?

(2 continued) after the coming of Christ that I deliver these records into the hands of my son; and it supposeth me that he will witness the entire destruction of my people.

[Mormon *supposes* Moroni will witness the entire destruction of his people, but it's not a sure thing. This destruction is still in the future at Cumorah. He is giving as much of the record as he has completed to Moroni at some location far from Cumorah, perhaps years ahead of the final battle.]

(2 continued) But may God grant that he may survive them,

[Mormon hopes Moroni will survive the final destruction of his people.]

(2 continued) that he may write somewhat concerning them, and somewhat concerning Christ,

[Mormon doesn't write directly to Moroni, but he writes about Moroni in the third person. This musing on Mormon's part suggests he is not giving the plates containing the Words of Mormon to Moroni. I infer from this that Mormon doesn't think Moroni will even see these comments. He is sealing the small plates with a prayer. He also hopes Moroni will write about his people and about Christ, but says nothing about Moroni adding to his, Mormon's, record.]

(2 continued) that perhaps some day it may profit them.

[If Moroni survives the destruction of Mormon's people, how would Moroni's writings profit those people? Perhaps Mormon hopes some of his people will survive along with Moroni.]

3 And now, I speak somewhat concerning that which I have written; for after I had made an abridgment from the plates of Nephi, down to the reign of this king Benjamin, of whom Amaleki spake,

[Mormon abridged the plates of Nephi down to the reign of King Benjamin. This abridgment is the Book of Lehi that Joseph dictated to Martin Harris in the spring of 1828. Harris lost the manuscript and Joseph did not resume the translation in earnest until April 1829 when Oliver Cowdery came to Harmony. Of course, the Lord told Joseph not to retranslate the Book of Lehi. At this time—when he gives the record he "has been making" to Moroni, he has only completed his abridgment called the Book of Lehi. He has a long way to go.]

(3 continued) I searched

[Something prompted him to search for the "small plates." Pres. Packer suggested it was reading Benjamin's description to his sons that led Mormon to return to Jashon to find these small plates. This means Mormon was already abridging the records when his armies went to Jashon; i.e., he got the records when he was 24 years old, and returned to Jashon as military leader when he was 34.]

(3 continued) among the records which had been delivered into my hands,

[Presumably these are the records Ammaron gave him charge over, as described in Mormon 1:3-4 and 4:23. This is a substantial collection of records as Brigham Young and others described. See Chapter 13 about the Repository.]

(3 continued) and I found these plates, which contained this small account of the prophets, from Jacob down to the reign of this king Benjamin, and also many of the words of Nephi.

[This "small account" is what we have today as 1 Nephi through Omni. They are usually called the "Small Plates of Nephi" because of this passage and 1 Nephi 9:2-4. In the context of the Book of Mormon, I think of them as the *original* plates of Nephi—the Fayette plates—as opposed to the large plates of Nephi that Mormon abridged.]

4 And the things which are upon these plates pleasing me,

[The next section is a parenthetical explanation of why the contents of the small plates pleased Mormon]

(4 continued) because of the prophecies of the coming of Christ; and my fathers knowing that many of them have been fulfilled; yea, and I also know that as many things as have been prophesied concerning us down to this day have been fulfilled, and as many as go beyond this day must surely come to pass—

[From his vantage point in the future, Mormon has seen the fulfillment of Nephi's prophecies, and he knows they will continue to be fulfilled in the future. Imagine Mormon reading about the European discovery of America, the war of Independence, the founding of the Constitution, etc.]

5 Wherefore, I choose these things,

[i.e., the things which are upon the small (or original) plates of Nephi. He's referring to the contents, not the physical plates, which is why he used the term *things* in both passages. Verses 4 and 5 both start by referring to *things*, plural. Note that Royal Skousen says *chose* here should be *choose*, present tense, as it probably was on the original manuscript. I agree, so I wrote it this way here. It's an important distinction because it puts the choice in the present tense; i.e., Mormon is choosing these things to emphasize as he finishes the rest of his abridgment, which he will do in the future.]

(5 continued) to finish my record upon them,

[Mormon is not literally writing his record on the small plates—Amaleki explained those plates were full (Omni 1:30)—but he is finishing his record *upon* the prophecies recorded on the small plates. It's another way of saying that Nephi's prophecies are the basis for the rest of his abridgement. Mormon chooses *these things*—these prophecies—to finish his record *upon* the prophecies, which will guide his editorial decisions for the remainder of his abridgement as he shows the fulfillment of the prophecies on the small plates.]

(5 continued) which remainder of my record I shall take from the plates of Nephi;

[Mormon uses the future tense to explain he has yet to complete the rest of the abridgment. Ammaron told Mormon to take the plates of Nephi and engrave on those plates the things he has observed during his life (Mormon 1:4). That means Mormon recorded history as it happened. Later, Mormon began the abridgment of the large plates. By the time he wrote Words of Mormon, he had only completed the abridgment through the reign of King Benjamin. We call these historical records the Large Plates of Nephi to distinguish them from the small plates (which I call the Fayette plates). None of the large plates were translated by Joseph Smith.]

(5 continued) and I cannot write the hundredth part of the things of my people.

[Mormon emphasizes how selective he has to be, which is why he found the small plates so helpful in the editorial process.]

6 But behold, I shall take these plates, which contain these prophesyings and revelations,

[This description clarifies that he's referring to the small plates, meaning the original plates of Nephi, which were not part of the plates Ammaron told him to take.]

(6 continued) and put them with the remainder of my record,

[Mormon put the small plates with the remainder of his record so he could refer to them as he continued his abridgment. A key question is the meaning of the phrase "put them with" in this context. Does it mean Mormon attached the small plates to his abridgement as many people assume? Did he punch holes in them and open the rings and add them? Nowhere does he state or imply that. As explained under verse 10 below, he simply *put* the small plates *with* his abridgement; i.e., he had them nearby.]

(6 continued) for they are choice unto me; and I know they will be choice unto my brethren.

[Mormon knows they will be choice unto *his brethren*, suggesting there are still some of his contemporaries for whom he has hope. He's keeping the plates with him as he's traveling around. Maybe he used them in his sermon (Moroni 7).

7 And I do this for a wise purpose; for thus it whispereth me, according to the workings of the Spirit of the Lord which is in me. And now, I do not know all things; but the Lord knoweth all things which are to come; wherefore, he worketh in me to do according to his will.

[This passage is often assumed to foreshadow the loss of the 116 pages, but in the context of what he had just written, it makes more sense that Mormon is referring to the inspiration he felt to (i) search for the small plates and (ii) use them to guide the rest of his abridgment; i.e., to write upon (about) the prophecies. The Spirit was telling Mormon to use the small plates to guide the rest of his abridgment. That these plates provided a replacement for the 116 pages is fortunate, and no doubt part of the plan, but there could have been many duplicate records in case some other part of Joseph's translation was lost. Perhaps Mormon also set aside the records of Limhi, for example. If Martin had not lost the 116 pages, we would never have known about these small plates.]

8 And my prayer to God is concerning my brethren, that they may once again come to the knowledge of God, yea, the redemption of Christ; that they may once again be a delightsome people.

[He's still praying for his contemporaries (he referred to them as *my brethren* many times in the sermon in Moroni 7). He *supposes* Moroni will see the entire destruction, but he still has hope for them and prays they can be delightsome again.]

9 And now I, Mormon, proceed to finish out my record, which I take from the plates of Nephi; and I make it

according to the knowledge and the understanding which God has given me.

[Now he's going to finish out his record. Presumably he's still "about to give" Moroni the portion of his abridgment he has completed up to this point. He wrote this note as a sort of title page or explanatory page for the small plates, showing why he kept them out of the repository while he works on his abridgment. It is possible he made similar annotations on other records that he used directly, such as Alma's discourses. These would still be in the repository of Nephite records, just as the small plates were until a messenger retrieved them to take to Fayette.]

10 Wherefore, it came to pass that after Amaleki had delivered up these plates into the hands of king Benjamin, he took them and put them with the other plates, which contained records which had been handed down by the kings, from generation to generation until the days of king Benjamin.

[Here's where we understand the meaning of the phrase "put them with" the other plates. Benjamin *put* the small plates *with* the large plates, but that does not mean he attached them. After all, Mormon had the large plates, but he still had to search for the small plates. They were not attached to the large plates. In plain English, the phrase *put them with* does not mean to *attach* them. It means to put them in proximity, next to, or together. It's the same meaning we find in Ezekiel 37:19. No connotation of the Hebrew means to attach; instead, it means to place nearby, next to, on top of, adjacent to, etc. See Appendix 4 for more detailed analysis.]

11 And they were handed down from king Benjamin, from generation to generation until they have fallen into my hands. And I, Mormon, pray to God that they may be preserved from this time henceforth. And I know that they will be preserved; for there are great things written upon them, out of which my people and their brethren shall be judged at the great and last day, according to the word of God which is written.

Whatever Happened to the Golden Plates?

[Verse 11 is Mormon's "title page" for the small plates. The plates haven't really "fallen into" Mormon's hands; he had to search for them. But now he prays that they will be preserved from this time henceforth; in fact, he *knows* they will be preserved. This is another indication he did not give them to Moroni. He prays that Moroni will survive his people, but he doesn't *know* that, not in the same way he *knows* the small plates will be preserved. That's because he's giving his abridgment to Moroni, but he's keeping the small plates in the repository, which he knows will be safe.

This is another indication that Mormon was using the small plates going forward to preach repentance; if he was just giving them to Moroni for the future, his people could not then be judged out of them. Mormon likely wrote Words of Mormon during the time when the Lord commanded him to preach to the people again (Mormon 3:2). Maybe it was during this period when he gave the Moroni 7 sermon.

As I mentioned, Mormon may have annotated many of the other records in the repository. The small plates duplicated the lost 116 pages, or close enough, even though they didn't replace the first two chapters of Mosiah. Our loss. But the Lord may have led Mormon to keep out several specific records, such as the sermons of Alma and Limhi's records, in case other parts of the abridgment—the *original* Book of Mormon, as Joseph put it— were lost.]

12 And now, concerning this king Benjamin—he had somewhat of contentions among his own people.

[Transition or bridge to the Book of Mosiah, as explained in the next section, probably dictated by Joseph Smith based on what he knew from the Book of Lehi.]

13 And it came to pass also that the armies of the Lamanites came down out of the land of Nephi, to battle against his people. But behold, king Benjamin gathered together his armies, and he did stand against them; and he did fight with the strength of his own arm, with the sword of Laban.

[The first verse of page 117, the material Joseph retained when Harris took the 116 pages. See D&C 10:41. This flows directly into what is now Mosiah chapter 1.]

If, as I propose here, Mormon was thinking of his contemporary brethren, then why did he proceed to finish out his record with the summary of king Benjamin's activities?

The most likely reason is that he didn't.

For many years, scholars have tried to make sense of the idea that Mormon would have written a transition from his own Words of Mormon, written around 400 A.D., to the current Book of Mosiah. The proposed solutions seemed contorted.

Now that we have the printer's manuscript to examine, we can see that our Mosiah Chapter 1 was almost certainly Chapter 3 in the original translation, meaning most of the first two chapters were on the lost 116 pages and we can make educated guesses about what was on page 117.

The bottom line: Words of Mormon originally ended with the current verse 11. Verse 12 was probably a transition provided by Joseph (who knew what was on the lost manuscript), and verses 13-18 were originally part of the Book of Mosiah.

In other words, the lost 116 pages included the first two chapters of the original Book of Mosiah. Page 117, which Joseph retained, began with our current verse 13.

An article in *BYU Studies* makes this case in some detail.[100] It's an excellent article that I recommend because it includes

---

[100] Jack M. Lyon and Kent R. Minson, "When Pages Collide: Dissecting the Words of Mormon," *BYU Studies*, 51:4 (2012), available online at https://byustudies.byu.edu/content/when-pages-collide-dissecting-words-mormon. A contrary view that suggests there was no page 117 retained by Joseph is Brant Gardner, "When Hypotheses Collide: Responding to Lyon and Minson's 'When Pages Collide,'" *Interpreter: A Journal of Mormon Scripture* 5

Royal Skousen's discussion of the gatherings used for the original manuscript.

The article follows the traditional order of translation, as I discussed in Chapter 9a. I won't get into the detail—you should read the article—but resolving the question about the transition between the Words of Mormon and the Book of Mosiah helps support the idea that the small plates were a separate record.

Regardless of the reason for the short gathering, it appears that there was at least some translated material Harris did not take with him.

> D&C 10:41 shows that Joseph had translated more than the 116 pages he gave to Martin Harris: "You shall translate the engravings which are on the [small] plates of Nephi, down even till you come to the reign of king Benjamin, or until you come to that which you have translated, *which you have retained*" (emphasis added). What he had retained was the end of Mosiah chapter 2 (which is now Words of Mormon verses 12–18) and perhaps more. Why did he retain it? Probably because it was written in the next gathering of manuscript pages, which, at the time, was only partially filled.[101]

This analysis leaves open the question of why they started another gathering instead of adding a sixth sheet to the fifth gathering, but we'll probably never know why—unless the manuscript is recovered some day. And it may have been an earlier gathering that was short one sheet.

According to this theory, the sixth gathering (designated by Skousen as A6) would have included some of the material from the first part of Mosiah.

I agree with the reasoning as far as it goes, but because the authors assume the small plates were attached somehow to the abridged plates, the case isn't as strong as it would otherwise be.

Look at how the narrative flows:

(2013): 105-119, online at http://www.mormoninterpreter.com/when-hypotheses-collide-responding-to-lyon-and-minsons-when-pages-collide/.
[101] Ibid.

9 And now I, Mormon, **proceed to finish out my record**, which I take from the plates of Nephi; and I make it according to the knowledge and the understanding which God has given me.

10 Wherefore, it came to pass that after Amaleki had delivered **up these plates** into the hands of king Benjamin, he took them **and put them with the other plates**, which contained records which had been handed down by the kings, from generation to generation until the days of king Benjamin.

11 And they were handed down from king Benjamin, from generation to generation until they have fallen into my hands. **And I, Mormon, pray to God that they may be preserved from this time henceforth. And I know that they will be preserved; for there are great things written upon them, out of which my people and their brethren shall be judged at the great and last day, according to the word of God which is written.**

If Mormon was sealing the small plates with what is effectively his title page, this is the natural ending place.

But instead of ending there, the text continues with a parenthetical bridge—verse 12—and then a historical narrative similar to the rest of Mormon's account. It is completely different from the preceding 11 verses. Instead, it flows organically into Chapter 1 of Mosiah.

13 And it came to pass also that the armies of the Lamanites came down out of the land of Nephi, to battle against his people. But behold, king Benjamin gathered together his armies, and he did stand against them; and he did fight with the strength of his own arm, with the sword of Laban.

14 And in the strength of the Lord they did contend against their enemies, until they had slain many thousands of the Lamanites. And it came to pass that they did contend against the Lamanites until they had driven them out of all the lands of their inheritance.

15 And it came to pass that after there had been false Christs, and their mouths had been shut, and they punished according to their crimes;

16 And after there had been false prophets, and false preachers and teachers among the people, and all these having been

punished according to their crimes; and after there having been much contention and many dissensions away unto the Lamanites, behold, it came to pass that king Benjamin, with the assistance of the holy prophets who were among his people—
17 For behold, king Benjamin was a holy man, and he did reign over his people in righteousness; and there were many holy men in the land, and they did speak the word of God with power and with authority; and they did use much sharpness because of the stiffneckedness of the people—
18 Wherefore, with the help of these, king Benjamin, by laboring with all the might of his body and the faculty of his whole soul, and also the prophets, did once more establish peace in the land.

We don't have the original manuscript for this part of the text, but we do have the printer's manuscript. There, the Book of Mosiah originally began at the end of what is now Words of Mormon 1: 18, designated by a dash and the words Chapter III, followed by another dash, and then what we now know as Mosiah 1:1.

An unidentified person crossed out the last two numerals, making it Chapter 1. From this, scholars infer that the 116 pages included the first two chapters of Mosiah. These chapters presumably started with an account of King Mosiah, which is why the book is named that way.

On the printer's manuscript, the phrase "the Book of Mosiah" is inserted above the line. The note in the Joseph Smith Papers says, "possibly inserted after the time of the original inscription." However, it is in Oliver's handwriting.

John Tvendtnes observed:

> Joseph Smith may have chosen to place the title "Book of Mosiah" in its current place because Mosiah 1:1 is where he took up the story after turning over the 116 pages to Martin Harris. If this is true, then Words of Mormon 1:12-18 evidently represent part of the record already translated before the loss of the 116 pages. Joseph may have retained this part (cf. D&C 10:41) because it was on a page which had not yet been filled. The book of Mosiah, in this case, was probably named after the first Mosiah,

whose history would have been part of the lost pages; otherwise, one might expect the book to be named after Benjamin. But this is by no means certain.[102]

Joseph was instructed to translate the plates of Nephi—what we now call the "small plates of Nephi"—"down even till you come to the reign of king Benjamin" (D&C 10:41). That seems to be what he did here.

I have done more detailed analysis of the phrase "put them with" by comparing it with the phrase in Ezekiel 37:15-19. If you are interested in more detail you can obtain access to my extra material by sending an email to lostzarahemla@gmail.com. Write "Put them with" in the subject line.

---

[102] John A. Tvedtnes, "Book Review of Jerald and Sandra Tanner's Covering Up the Black Hole in the Book of Mormon," in *Review of Books on the Book of Mormon*, Vol. 3 1991, pp. 201-203, online here: http://publications.mi.byu.edu/fullscreen/?pub=1426&index=19.

Whatever Happened to the Golden Plates?

Figure 4 - Diagram of Two Sets of Plates

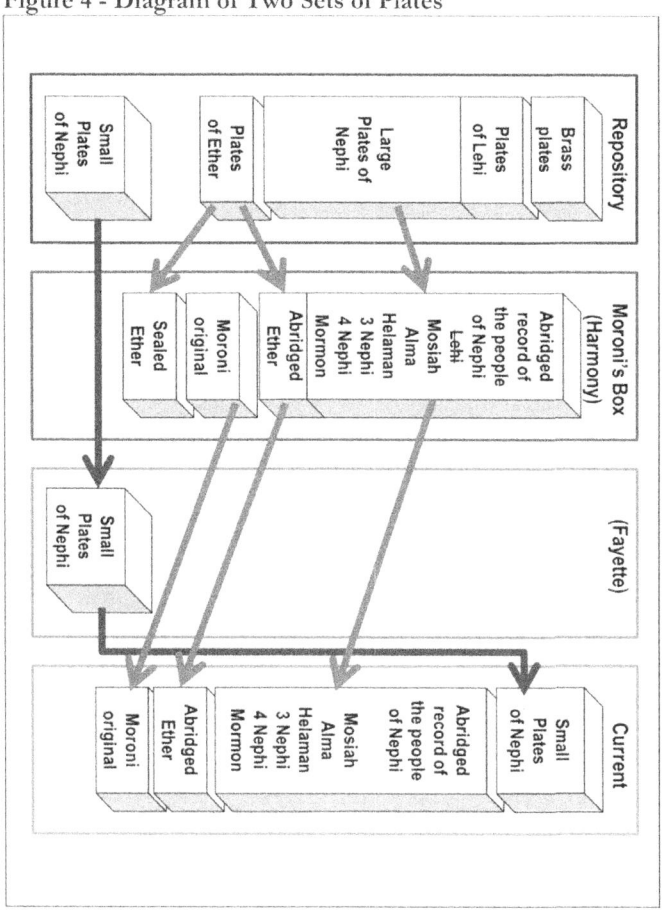

12 Mormon's Repository

Mormon 6:6 describes the repository of Nephite records:

6 And it came to pass that when we had gathered in all our people in one to the land of Cumorah, behold I, Mormon, began to be old; and knowing it to be the last struggle of my people, and having been commanded of the Lord that I should not suffer the records which had been handed down by our fathers, which were sacred, to fall into the hands of the Lamanites, (for the Lamanites would destroy them) therefore I made this record out of the plates of Nephi, **and hid up in the hill Cumorah all the records which had been entrusted to me by the hand of the Lord**, save it were these few plates which I gave unto my son Moroni.

I think the hill Cumorah Mormon referred to here is the same hill in New York where Moroni buried the abridgment. The small plates of Nephi—the Fayette plates—remained there, where Mormon put them, until a divine messenger retrieved them in 1829 and took them to Fayette to be translated. The Harmony plates—the original Book of Mormon that Moroni deposited in the box of stone and cement—were returned by a divine messenger to this repository when Joseph finished translating them in Harmony.

Orson Pratt made this point when he stated,

When Moroni, about thirty-six years after, made the deposit of the book entrusted to him, he was, without doubt, inspired to select **a department of the hill separate from the great sacred depository of the numerous volumes** hid up by his father.

The particular place in the hill, where Moroni secreted the book, was revealed, by the angel, to the Prophet Joseph Smith, to whom the volume was delivered in September, A.D. 1827. **But the grand repository of all the numerous records of the ancient**

nations of the western continent, was located in another department of the hill, and its contents under the charge of holy angels, until the day should come for them to be transferred to the sacred temple of Zion.

The hill Cumorah, with the surrounding vicinity, is distinguished as the great battle-field on which, and near which, two powerful nations were concentrated with all their forces, men, women, and children, and fought till hundreds of thousands on both sides were hewn down, and left to moulder upon the ground.[103]

Oliver Cowdery made the location of Cumorah clear in his unambiguous Letter VII, which was approved by Joseph Smith and reprinted multiple times while Joseph was alive and later.[104] Some have claimed that Joseph and Oliver never claimed specific revelation about the location of Cumorah, but what could be more convincing than actually entering the repository and seeing it for themselves?

The existence of the repository in the New York hill is far more significant than the stone box in which Moroni hid the plates for Joseph to find. It's one thing for a solitary Moroni to haul plates to New York from somewhere else on the continent (or from another continent). It's another thing altogether for that same solitary Moroni (or for his father Mormon) to haul wagon loads of plates and other artifacts from somewhere else on the continent, just to store them in the New York hill.

To put it another way, if the room where Mormon hid all the Nephite records (wagon loads of them) was in New York, then Oliver Cowdery had good reason to write that it was a fact that the final battles also took place there—even if he didn't receive a specific revelation to that effect. And, in that case,

---

[103] Orson Pratt, "The Hill Cumorah; or the sacred depository of wisdom and understanding," *The Latter-Day Saints' Millennial Star*, July 7, 1866. Online at http://www.lettervii.com/2016/08/the-hill-cumorah-sacred-depository.html.

[104] A collection of republications is available at http://www.lettervii.com/.

Joseph Smith had good reason for endorsing and incorporating Oliver's account.

Cameron Packer wrote an excellent article[105] on the topic that includes ten references to the room of records. The Abstract explains:

> The significance of the Hill Cumorah in the restoration of the gospel goes beyond its identification as the ancient repository of the metal plates known as the Book of Mormon. In the second half of the 19th century, a teaching about a cave in the hill began surfacing in the writings of several leaders of the Church of Jesus Christ of Latter-day Saints. In their view, the hill was not only the place where Joseph Smith received the plates but also their final repository, along with other sacred treasures, after the translation was finished. This article cites ten different accounts, all secondhand, that refer to this cave and what was found there. The author includes a comparison of the accounts that discusses additional records in the cave, God's dominion over Earth's treasure, miraculous dealings of God, and the significance of the presence of the sword of Laban.

In his footnote 1, Cameron observes that Orson Pratt's article about the two compartments was not his only discussion of Cumorah in New York.

> Orson Pratt often referred to the cave in Cumorah but not with specific reference to Joseph Smith and others entering to return the plates. One of Pratt's accounts is cited in this article. Several of the other references to the cave that are not included in this article are found in Journal of Discourses, 14:330–31; 15:182–83; 16:57; 17:30–31; 17:281; 19:218. **Another source for Pratt's accounts is supposedly the Quorum of the Twelve Minutes, 6 May 1849**, but I have not been able to confirm this. Brigham

---

[105] Cameron J. Packer, "Cumorah's Cave," Journal of Book of Mormon Studies 13/1-2 (2004): 50-57, 170-71. Online at
http://publications.mi.byu.edu/publications/jbms/13/1/S00006-50bc6ae14cf1b5Packer.pdf

Young's record of that date, however, is interesting to note: "I met with President Willard Richards and the Twelve on the 6th. We spent the time in interesting conversation upon old times, Joseph, **the plates, Mount Cumorah, treasures and records known to be hid in the earth,** the gift of seeing, and how Joseph obtained his first seer stone" (Manuscript History of Brigham Young, 6 May 1849, Church Archives). See also *Journal History of The Church of Jesus Christ of Latter-day Saints*, 6 May 1849.

Orson Pratt often made affirmative statements without clearly explaining whether they were speculative or factual. For example, he often spoke of Lehi landing in Chile, even after Joseph Smith edited out Pratt's geography speculation when he wrote the Wentworth letter. However, when he added geography footnotes to the 1879 Book of Mormon, Pratt was careful to distinguish between speculative ideas, such as the landing in Chile and the location of Zarahemla, and declarative statements such as the location of Cumorah in New York.

Brigham Young gave the most extensive public comment about the repository on June 17, 1877, at a conference in Farmington. He said

> I lived right in the country where the plates were found from which the Book of Mormon was translated, and I know a great many things pertaining to that country.
>
> I believe I will take the liberty to tell you of another circumstance that will be as marvelous as anything can be. **This is an incident in the life of Oliver Cowdery, but he did not take the liberty of telling such things in meeting as I take.**
>
> I tell these things to you, and I have a motive for doing so. **I want to carry them to the ears of my brethren and sisters, and to the children also, that they may grow to an understanding of some things that seem to be entirely hidden from the human family.**
>
> **Oliver Cowdery went with the Prophet Joseph when he deposited these plates.** Joseph did not translate all of the plates;

there was a portion of them sealed, which you can learn from the Book of Doctrine and Covenants.

When Joseph got the plates, the angel instructed him to carry them back to the hill Cumorah, which he did. Oliver says that when Joseph and Oliver went there, the hill opened, and they walked into a cave, **in which there was a large and spacious room.** He says he did not think, at the time, whether they had the light of the sun or artificial light; but that it was just as light as day.

They laid the plates on a table; it was a large table that stood in the room. Under this table there was a pile of plates as much as two feet high, and there were altogether in this room **more plates than probably many wagon loads**; they were piled up in the corners and along the walls.

The first time they went there the sword of Laban hung upon the wall; but when they went again it had been taken down and laid upon the table across the gold plates; it was unsheathed, and on it was written these words: "This sword will never be sheathed again until the kingdoms of this world become the kingdom of our God and his Christ."

I tell you this as coming not only from Oliver Cowdery, but others who were familiar with it, and who understood it just as well as we understand coming to this meeting, enjoying the day, and by and by we separate and go away, forgetting most of what is said, but remembering some things.

So is it with other circumstances in life. **I relate this to you, and I want you to understand it.** I take this liberty of referring to those things **so that they will not be forgotten and lost.**

Carlos Smith was a young man of as much veracity as any young man we had, and **he was a witness to these things.** Samuel Smith saw some things, Hyrum saw a good many things, but Joseph was the leader.

Now, you may think I am unwise in publicly telling these things, thinking perhaps I should preserve them in my own breast; but such is not my mind. **I would like the people called Latter-day Saints to understand some little things with regard to the workings and dealings of the Lord with his people here upon the earth.** I could relate to you a great many more, all of which are familiar to many of our brethren and sisters (emphasis added).[106]

Brigham Young had discussed this repository on previous occasions, but here he decided to make it public. He noted that Oliver didn't talk about this in public, and we have no record that Joseph or the others did, but Brigham was concerned that the knowledge of this room would be forgotten and lost, so he had it put on record in the *Journal of Discourses*.

Two points stand out. First, there was a table with records and artifacts on it, similar to what David Whitmer described. The other accounts listed by Cameron relate similar details. This was a real, physical experience.

Second, there were "more plates than probably many wagon loads." Item 6 in the article, a journal entry by Jesse Nathaniel Smith from February 1874, relates that Brigham Young "said there was great wealth in the room in sacred implements, vestments, arms, precious metals and precious stones, more than a six-mule team could draw." Heber C. Kimball (Item 2) said Joseph and others "saw more records than ten men could carry."

These comments suggest that Joseph, Oliver and the others mentioned may have moved the plates from the repository in Cumorah.

When asked where the plates are now, David Whitmer said they were in New York, not in Cumorah, "but not far away from that place." This indicates that he knew where they were. How could he know unless he helped move the plates and other artifacts, or was told by those who did move them?

---

[106] Available online at http://jod.mrm.org/19/36.

Whatever Happened to the Golden Plates?

Mormon moved the records to Cumorah from the hill Shim. Perhaps Joseph and the others moved them back to the hill Shim to protect them from the "Rochester adventurers" David spoke of when he said, "when they [the plates] are translated much useful information will be brought to light. But till that day arrives, no Rochester adventurers shall ever see them or the treasures."[107]

Consider the evidence. We have multiple second-hand accounts of Joseph, Oliver, and others entering a room in the New York Hill Cumorah that was full of additional plates and other artifacts. Although second-hand, these accounts were related by people who knew Oliver and Joseph very well. Brigham Young gave the most explicit description just two months before he died, emphasizing that he related the events "so that they will not be forgotten and lost."

Around 2006, a man-made room was discovered in the Hill that matches the description given by Brigham Young and the others. Whether or not it was Mormon's repository, it shows that a room can be built in the hill and concealed there. The room was empty of artifacts, which we expect based on what David and Oliver said about the plates no longer being in the Hill Cumorah (although David said they were not far from there).

We have Oliver writing in Letter VII that the final battles of the Nephites took place in the valley west of the New York Hill Cumorah. We have Joseph Smith endorsing Oliver's account and incorporating it into his own journal. We have multiple reprintings of Oliver's account while Joseph was alive. We have Joseph alluding to the Hill Cumorah in D&C 128.

---

[107] Edward Stevenson, *Reminiscences of Joseph the Prophet and the Coming Forth of the Book of Mormon* (1877), page 14, online at
https://archive.org/stream/reminiscencesofj00stev#page/n17/mode/2up.

The simplest explanation is that the final battles of the Jaredites and Nephites took place in the valley west of the New York Hill Cumorah, just as Oliver wrote. This simple explanation also reconciles the available evidence.

Compare that to the series of assumptions required for the two-Cumorah theory. First, that the multiple accounts of Joseph, Oliver, and others entering the room on multiple occasions are all visionary experiences. Second, that it is impossible to have a room in the New York Hill Cumorah. Third, that Oliver was merely speculating about the scene of the final battles, and that when he wrote it was a fact, he was lying or confused or inarticulate. Fourth, when Joseph endorsed and incorporated Oliver's Letter VII, he, too, was speculating.

I choose the simplest explanation. Others choose the complex explanation. I have no problem with whatever you choose, as readers here, so long as we are all clear on what our choices entail.

In my view, the multiple accounts of multiple people making multiple visits to the room in the New York Hill Cumorah that contained wagon loads of plates and other artifacts effectively corroborate Letter VII. And with Letter VII putting Cumorah in New York, we can work out Book of Mormon geography from there.

13 Handing them over

There are a few seemingly contradictory accounts of what happened to the plates when Joseph completed the translation. I suggest the accounts can be best reconciled by the two-sets-of-plates theory.

The best-known is Joseph Smith – History 1:60:

> I soon found out the reason why I had received such strict charges to keep them safe, and why it was that the messenger had said that when I had done what was required at my hand, **he would call for them**. For no sooner was it known that I had them, than the most strenuous exertions were used to get them from me. Every stratagem that could be invented was resorted to for that purpose. The persecution became more bitter and severe than before, and multitudes were on the alert continually to get them from me if possible. But by the wisdom of God, they remained safe in my hands, **until I had accomplished by them what was required at my hand.** When, according to arrangements, **the messenger called for them, I delivered them up to him; and he has them in his charge until this day,** being the second day of May, one thousand eight hundred and thirty-eight.

A key phrase here is "according to arrangements." Joseph made arrangements to give the plates to the heavenly messenger before he left Harmony. The arrangements included receiving plates to translate in Fayette. In this sense, Joseph fulfilled his obligation for the original set of plates in May 1829, before leaving Harmony.

But he still had the Fayette plates to translate.

Assuming a messenger brought the small plates of Nephi from the repository, what did Joseph do with them?

Brigham Young says that "When Joseph got the plates, the angel instructed him to carry them back to the hill Cumorah, which he did." This statement could not refer to the Harmony plates because Joseph gave those to a messenger before he left Harmony. It was the *messenger* on the road to Fayette who took those plates to Cumorah.

Around the time Joseph finished the Fayette translation, the Three Witnesses saw the angel and the plates. These could have been the Harmony plates or the Fayette plates or both; the descriptions are not specific enough to tell. In 1884, David said that "the angel took the Record, and turned the leaves, and showed it to us by the power of God. They were taken away by the angel to a cave, which we saw by the power of God while we were yet in the Spirit."[108] This could mean they saw the cave in vision at that time, or they later visited the cave in Cumorah while still "in the spirit." Either way, Joseph did not return the plates to Cumorah at this point.

A few days after his experience with the Three Witnesses, Joseph showed a set of plates to the Eight Witnesses in the Palmyra area. These witnesses did not specifically describe the plates. They could have been the Harmony or the Fayette plates.

But where did they come from?

According to his mother, Joseph met one of the three Nephites who gave him the plates to show to the eight witnesses, but she doesn't say where. The likely meeting place was the repository on Cumorah.

As mentioned in JS-H, quoted above, Joseph "delivered them up to" the messenger when he was finished with them. I think this means he took them back to the repository. Separately, David Whitmer said the angel returned the plates to "a cave" after showing them to the Three Witnesses.

Other isolated accounts may refer to the Harmony plates. In 1834, Joseph Smith was interviewed by Peter Bauder, who

---

[108] *The Saints' Herald*, 21 June 1884, *Interviews*, p. 127.

reported that "after he [Joseph] had a part translated, the angel commanded him to carry the plate [sic] into a certain piece of woods, which he did:—the angel took them and carried them to parts unknown to him."[109] This statement parallels Martin Harris' claim that he translated a third of the *first part* of the translation. It suggests that this is how Joseph gave the plates to the messenger before leaving Harmony. If Joseph did not know where the angel was taking them, he learned it when they encountered the messenger on the trip to Fayette who was taking the plates to Cumorah. As discussed previously, this may have come as a shock to Joseph and explains why he turned pale, as David Whitmer described.

In Nauvoo, Joseph is reported to have said in 1842 that "Those plates are not now in this country… they were exhibited to a few at first for the sake of obtaining their testimony—no others have ever seen them—and they will never again be exhibited."[110] Presumably the visitor wanted to see them; Joseph explained the plates were not in the area where he lived—the country around Nauvoo.

In his 1881 *Chicago Times* interview, David said, "After the plates had been translated, which process required about six months, the same heavenly visitant appeared and reclaimed the gold tablets of the ancient people, informing Smith that he would replace them with other records of the lost tribes that had been brought with them during their wanderings from the Asia, which would be forthcoming when the world was ready to receive them."[111] This statement is anomalous; it took Joseph only 3 months (April-June 1829) to translate the current Book of Mormon. Perhaps David was adding up all the time spent translating in Fayette (in 1828 with Martin Harris and in 1829 with Emma and Oliver), after which Joseph gave the plates to

---

[109] *OTH* #17, p. 123.
[110] OTH, #27, p. 126-7.
[111] OTH #86, p. 150

the angel who promised to deliver plates to Joseph in Fayette. Could the small plates of Nephi be considered "other records of the lost tribes?" Possibly. Otherwise, these "other records" never materialized.

14 Whatever Happened to the Golden Plates?

As discussed previously, at a Church conference in Ohio in October 1831, Hyrum asked Joseph to explain how the Book of Mormon came forth. The Minutes read:

> Br. Hyrum Smith said that he thought best that the information of the coming forth of the book of Mormon be related by Joseph himself to the Elders present that all might know for themselves. Br. Joseph Smith jr. said that it was not intended to tell the world all the particulars of the coming forth of the book of Mormon, & also said that it was not expedient for him to relate these things &c."[112]

Most authors interpret this statement to refer to the *translation* of the Book of Mormon, but I think this is a mistake. That's not what Joseph said. Joseph referred to "the *particulars of the coming forth* of the Book of Mormon." That would include more than just the translation.

Recall that all 11 official witnesses were present at that meeting. If Joseph meant it was "not intended" to tell the world the "particulars" of the *translation*, then several of these men, including the Three Witnesses, violated his instructions when they described details of the translation. It seems unlikely to me that they would publicly discuss something Joseph told them not to discuss.

For that reason, I propose that Joseph was referring to the acquisition and disposition of the two sets of plates. After all, by

---

[112] *Minutes*, 25-26 October 1831, available online at http://www.josephsmithpapers.org/paper-summary/minutes-25-26-october-1831/4.

1831 the story of Joseph finding and translating the plates was well known, published in numerous newspapers. The testimonies of the witnesses were included in every copy of the Book of Mormon. But there were "particulars" about these events that Joseph did not want to be published.

True, beginning in 1834 Oliver wrote (with Joseph's assistance) more details about the discovery of the plates in his eight letters which were published in the *Messenger and Advocate* and reprinted in the 1841 *Times and Seasons* and *Gospel Reflector*. In 1842 the *Times and Seasons* published Joseph's official history. But these accounts merely provided an official version of events that had long been public knowledge; i.e., Joseph found a set of gold plates translated them, and returned them to the angel who has charge of them today.

Nothing for people to search for.

If, as I propose, he and Hyrum and the others had moved the plates to the hill Shim or another location, Joseph would not want to attract public attention to that fact. Better to say nothing in public.

In my view, Joseph would have good reason not to make public the existence of two sets of plates because of what it meant in terms of the records repository. If, as Joseph said privately, it contained "tons of choice treasures & records," then surely he would not want to encourage treasure hunters to search for it. If the original set of plates was worth $1 million in today's money, the repository containing stacks of plates and other artifacts could be worth a billion dollars in modern terms.

It wasn't until the Saints were in Utah that Brigham Young talked publicly about the repository. By then, the furor over the plates had died down. As David Whitmer explained, the plates were no longer in the Hill Cumorah anyway.

Joseph understandably resorted to secrecy from the outset, when he prayed in secret in the Sacred Grove. His refusal to display the plates caused him difficulty with others from the time he first acquired them. It was one thing to tell people he had the plates and that they were in a box, but maybe seeing the actual plates—a million dollars' worth of gold in today's money—would have such an intoxicating effect that even his close associates would try to steal them.

Following their baptism, Joseph explained the importance of secrecy in Joseph Smith-History:

> 74 Our minds being now enlightened, we began to have the scriptures laid open to our understandings, and the true meaning and intention of their more mysterious passages revealed unto us in a manner which we never could attain to previously, nor ever before had thought of. In the meantime **we were forced to keep secret the circumstances of having received the Priesthood and our having been baptized**, owing to a spirit of persecution which had already manifested itself in the neighborhood.
>
> 75 We had been threatened with being mobbed, from time to time, and this, too, by professors of religion. And their intentions of mobbing us were only counteracted by the influence of my wife's father's family (under Divine providence), who had become very friendly to me, and who were opposed to mobs, and were willing that I should be allowed to continue the work of translation without interruption; and therefore offered and promised us protection from all unlawful proceedings, as far as in them lay.

In the face of this opposition and the constant harassment by those who wanted the plates, surely it was wise to keep away from the world the knowledge of the repository of plates and ancient treasure.

So whatever happened to the golden plates?

The original set of plates, the ones Moroni hid up in the box he made of stone and cement, were retrieved by Joseph Smith in 1827, translated in Harmony, and then returned to a heavenly messenger who returned them to the repository in Cumorah.

The second set of plates—the plates of Nephi described in D&C 10—were taken by a divine messenger to Fayette, where Joseph translated them. Most likely, he and Oliver returned them to the repository after showing them to the Eight Witnesses.

The remarks of President Anthony W. Ivins, which I quoted in the preliminary pages of this book, deserve serious consideration. He made these remarks in the April 1928 General Conference to commemorate the acquisition of the Hill Cumorah by the Church. He said these records

> and the other sacred records which were deposited in the hill Cumorah **still lie in their repository**, awaiting the time when the Lord shall see fit to bring them forth, that they may be published to the world.
>
> **Whether they have been removed from the spot where Mormon deposited them we cannot tell**, but this we know, that they are safe under the guardianship of the Lord, and that they will be brought forth at the proper time, as the Lord has declared they should be, for the benefit and blessing of the people of the world, for his word never fails....
>
> **Without doubt, these treasures lie concealed today, some of them, at least, to be brought forth in the not-distant future.** How soon this will be we do not know, but this is certain, we are more than a century nearer that time than we were at the time when Joseph Smith took from their resting place, in the hill Cumorah, the plates from which he translated the contents of the Book of Mormon.
>
> **All of these incidents to which I have referred, my brethren and sisters, are very closely associated with this particular spot in the state of New York.** Therefore I feel, as I said in the beginning of my remarks, that **the acquisition of that spot of ground is more than an incident in the history of the Church; it is an epoch—an epoch which in my opinion is fraught with**

that which may become of greater interest to the Latter-day Saints than that which has already occurred. We know that all of these records, all the sacred records of the Nephite people, were deposited by Mormon in that hill. That incident alone is sufficient to make it the sacred and hallowed spot that it is to us....

I bear witness to you that the words which I have read here, quoted from the Book of Mormon, which refer to the future will be fulfilled. **Those additional records will come forth, they will be published to the world, that the children of our Father may be converted to faith in Christ, our Lord and Redeemer, through obedience to the doctrines which he taught.** May God our Father hasten that day, is my humble prayer, and I ask it through Jesus Christ. Amen.

Is there any doubt that the coming forth of these additional records would "become of greater interest to the Latter-day Saints than that which has already occurred" at Cumorah?

I look forward to this day, which I think will arrive once members of the Church fully embrace the Book of Mormon and its teachings, along with the teachings of the modern prophets and apostles.

Appendix 1: Joseph Smith Papers

Today, the best source of historical information relating to Joseph Smith is the Joseph Smith Papers. I encourage everyone interested in Church history to buy the books or access the web page (or both). You'll find a wealth of original documents, as well as extensive and useful commentary.

(I like to tell people to throw away the old *History of the Church*, but of course I'm kidding. You need those to follow footnotes in Church-related publications. A few authors still cite *History of the Church*, but hopefully that won't continue because of all the problems with the way that series was compiled.)

The web address is easy to remember and find: http://www.josephsmithpapers.org/.

Many of the footnotes in this book include links to the Joseph Smith Papers.

The Papers are organized by category as follows:

- Documents (1913): Letters, revelations, reports of discourses, minutes, etc.

- Journals (10): Journals and diaries.

- Administrative Records (371): Minutes and other official records.

- Revelations and Translations (37): Early manuscript and printed versions of scriptural works.

- Histories (50): Early histories and draft material for the later History of the Church.

- Legal, Business, and Financial Records (147): Court, land and business papers.

The "Histories" category contains 50 items.[113] These histories in turn fall into four categories, as listed below.
- Joseph Smith Histories (6)
- Assigned Histories (11)
- History, 1838-1856 (Manuscript History of the Church) (30)
- Other Histories (3)

---

[113] You can see the list of items here:
http://www.josephsmithpapers.org/the-papers/histories

Appendix 2: Accounts of the 1829 Trip to Fayette

There must have been an important reason for the move to Fayette because it required miracles to bring about.

First was the striking commandment for Joseph to contact David Whitmer, having come by surprise through the Urim and Thummim.

David received miraculous help on his farm to enable him to make the two-day trip to Harmony in the middle of planting season.

Joseph Smith apparently experienced anxiety about the move to Fayette. Oliver Cowdery told David that Joseph Smith had tracked his, David's, entire trip. Oliver wrote down the names of the taverns where David stayed, the people he met, and other details. David was astonished because every detail was correct.

David repeated his experience encountering the divine messenger taking the plates to Cumorah several times.

To the extent scholars have paid attention to the 1829 trip to Fayette, they have generally expressed skepticism or even dismissed it as the product of David's faulty memory. For example, after citing the Pratt/Smith report, one LDS scholar wrote,

> This report would be much more conclusive had it not been recorded nearly fifty years later. The passage of time and the accepted designation of "Cumorah" as the name of the New York hill by the time of the recollection argue against this second-hand report from Whitmer as being a definitive statement.[114]

---

[114] Brant A. Gardner, *Traditions of the Fathers*, (Greg Kofford Books, 2015), pp. 375-6.

This effort to undermine David's credibility relies on the premise that David never related the account until 49 years after the fact. The scholarly motivation appears to be resistance to a New York Cumorah because of a preference for a Mesoamerican setting for the Book of Mormon.

Of course, we don't know that David did *not* relate the account of the messenger going to Cumorah with the plates much earlier. We just don't have a specific written account of that happening. However, when Edward Stevenson interviewed David in 1886 and asked about the incident, he was prompted to do so before he left Salt Lake City by Zina Young. Her only known contact with David Whitmer was in 1832 when he was one of the missionaries who converted her family. She would have had to learn about it back then, not long after David picked up Joseph and Oliver.[115]

It's also possible she read about the account when the *Deseret News* published the Pratt/Smith interview on 16 November 1878. In that case, though, one wonders why Stevenson would not have read or heard about the account from that publication. Stevenson makes no reference to the *Deseret News* version in his diary.

Stevenson wrote about his February 1886 interview in his diary, in a letter to Daniel H. Wells that was published in the *Millennial Star*, and in a letter to the Editor of the Utah Journal. In January 1887 Stevenson visited David again and wrote about it in his Journal, in an article published in the *Juvenile Instructor*, an article in the *Millennial Star*, and yet another article in the 1889 *Juvenile Instructor* that changed some of the details.

---

[115] I discussed this on my blog here http://bookofmormonwars.blogspot.com/2016/05/note-on-cumorah-david-whitmer-and-zina.html and here http://bookofmormonwars.blogspot.com/2016/05/more-on-david-whitmer-zina-young-and.html.

Whatever Happened to the Golden Plates?

The 7-8 September 1878 interview of David by Orson Pratt and Joseph F. Smith generated four known versions. Smith wrote about it in his journal. Pratt and Smith wrote a formal report to President John Taylor and the Council of the Twelve which was published in the *Deseret News* on Nov. 16, 1878. Orson Pratt wrote a private letter about the interview. In 1918, Smith spoke about the interview in a public meeting and recorded his thoughts in his journal.

Comparing these accounts is beyond the scope of this book, but they are all included in Lyndon W. Cook, *David Whitmer Interviews*, which I highly recommend. David's story about encountering the stranger carrying the plates to Cumorah is consistent each time he related it.

David was also adamant that Joseph had given the plates to a messenger before leaving Harmony. In 1881, he was interviewed by the *Kansas City Journal*. The article quoted David to say the following:

> Soon after I received another letter from Cowdery, telling me to come down into Pennsylvania and bring him and Joseph to my father's house, giving as a reason therefor that they had received a commandment from God to that effect. I went down to Harmony, and found everything just as they had written me. The next day after I got there **they packed up the plates** and we proceeded on our journey to my father's house where we arrived in due time, and the day after we commenced upon the translation of the remainder of the plates.[116] (emphasis added)

After this article was published, David wrote to the editor of the paper to complain about "several errors in the interview."

> In regard to my going to Harmony, my statement was that "I found everything as Cowdery had written me, and that they

---

[116] David Whitmer, as interviewed by the Kansas City Journal (1881), *Opening the Heavens*, p. 148.

packed up the next day and went to my father's, (**did not say 'packed up the plates'**) and that he, Smith, (not 'we') then commenced the translation of the remainder of the plates."[117]

David knew Joseph and Oliver did not pack up the plates because the man he encountered on the road to Fayette had them in his knapsack.

The phrase "the remainder of the plates" is vague; it could mean the plates of Nephi if they were attached to the Harmony plates (although that doesn't explain the Title Page), or it could mean the separate set of "plates of Nephi," meaning the Fayette plates, as I propose.

Appendix 3: The Lost 116 Pages

In Chapter 9a I discussed the order of translation and explained my approach to understanding what Martin Harris meant when he said he translated 1/3 of the first part of the translation. My detailed analysis is available at the website www.mobom.org.

Appendix 4: Mormon and the Small Plates

If, as I propose, Mormon put the small plates with his account to guide his editorial work and for the benefit of "his brethren," there should be evidence that the small plates did influence his own writing.

And there is.

---

[117] David Whitmer (1881), *Opening the Heavens*, p. 149.

For example, only in the sermon and in 1 Nephi 17:25 do we find the phrase "good thing" as a positive.

The concept of *searching diligently* appears only in Mormon's sermon, the small plates, once in 3 Nephi, and in Benjamin's counsel that may have prompted Mormon to search for the small plates in the first place.

Mormon: "Wherefore, I beseech of you, brethren, that ye should **search diligently** in the light of Christ that ye may know good from evil" (Moroni 7:19). "they had **searched the scriptures diligently**" (Alma 17:2, Mormon's abridgment).

Nephi: "Blessed art thou, Nephi, because of thy faith, for **thou hast sought me diligently**" (1 Nephi 2:19). "I, Nephi, was desirous also that I might see, and hear, and know of these things, by the power of the Holy Ghost, which is the gift of God unto all those who **diligently seek** him, as well in times of old as in the time that he should manifest himself unto the children of men… For he that **diligently seeketh** shall find" (1 Nephi 10:17, 19).

Enos: "I bear record that the people of Nephi did **seek diligently** to restore the Lamanites unto the true faith in God" (Enos 1:20).

Benjamin: I would that ye should remember to **search them diligently**, that ye may profit thereby (Mosiah 1:7).

Savior: "Yea, a commandment I give unto you that ye **search these things diligently**; for great are the words of Isaiah" (3 Nephi 23:1).

John Tvendtnes noted a likelihood that Mormon 7 and Words of Mormon were written about the same time.

Mormon's concluding remarks in Words of Mormon 1:11 reflect the thoughts he expressed in the last chapter he wrote in Mormon 7. He wrote of the preservation of the records (cf. Mormon 7:1) and of the judgment (cf. Mormon 7:6, 10). In Words of Mormon 1:8, he expressed the hope—also given in Mormon 7:5, 10—that his brethren might come to believe in Christ. This makes me wonder if the last part of Mormon (chapters 6-9) may have been written on the small plates. Indeed, Mormon 6:1 begins with the words, "And now I finish my record," which is reminiscent of

Words of Mormon 1:5, 9. In any event, the similarity of words found in Mormon 6-7 and in Words of Mormon 1:1-11 may indicate a temporal proximity of the writing of those two records.[118]

This timeframe is consistent with the analysis in Chapter 11, where I proposed that Mormon used these small plates of Nephi in his preaching well before he finished his abridgment.

Appendix 5: References on the Translation of the Book of Mormon

Many people have sought to harmonize the numerous accounts of the translation. In addition to the essay on lds.org mentioned in Chapter 5, I recommend the following three articles and a book.

Richard Lloyd Anderson, "By the Gift and Power of God," *Ensign*, September 1977, available online at https://www.churchofjesuschrist.org/study/ensign/1977/09/by-the-gift-and-power-of-god?lang=eng

Roger Nicholson, "The Spectacles, the Stone, the Hat, and the Book: A Twenty-first Century Believer's View of the Book of Mormon Translation," *Interpreter* 5 (2013): 121-190, available online at
http://www.mormoninterpreter.com/the-spectacles-the-stone-the-hat-and-the-book-a-twenty-first-century-believers-view-of-the-book-of-mormon-translation/;

---

[118] John A. Tvedtnes, "Book Review of Jerald and Sandra Tanner's Covering Up the Black Hole in the Book of Mormon," in *Review of Books on the Book of Mormon*, Vol. 3 1991, pp. 201-203

Whatever Happened to the Golden Plates?

John W. Welch, "The Miraculous Translation of the Book of Mormon," in *Opening the Heavens: Accounts of Divine Manifestations, 1820–1844*, ed. John W. Welch (Salt Lake City: Deseret Book; Provo, UT: Brigham Young University Press, 2005), 76–213, available online at https://byustudies.byu.edu/content/opening-heavens-miraculous-translation-book-mormon-chapter-only.

A book on this topic is Michael Hubbard MacKay and Gerrit J. Dirkmaat, *From Darkness unto Light: Joseph Smith's Translation and Publication of the Book of Mormon,* (Religious Studies Center, BYU, and Deseret Book 2015). I found this book useful in many respects, but I have reservations that I explain in my book review, which is available upon request at lostzarahemla@gmail.com. Write "Plates book reviews" in the subject line.

Jonathan Neville

Appendix 6: The Sequence of the Translation of the Book of Mormon

In Chapter 9a I quoted a portion of Richard Bushman's analysis of the sequence of events. Here is a more complete version of what he wrote.

> By May 1829, Joseph and Cowdery had not yet translated what are now the opening books of the Book of Mormon. After the loss of the 116 pages, Joseph did not begin again at the beginning. Joseph and Emma took up the translation where Joseph and Harris had broken off the previous June, that is, around the first part of the Book of Mosiah in the reign of King Benjamin. Joseph and Cowdery kept on in sequence. Sooner or later, Joseph had to decide what to do about the loss of the previous manuscript, containing the first four hundred years of Book of Mormon narrative. In May he received a revelation telling him not to retranslate…. [see D&C 10] In late May or June, probably after the rest of the book was done, he and Cowdery began work on 1 Nephi.[63]"[119]

I Nephi was translated from the unabridged plates of Nephi, commonly referred to as the "small plates of Nephi," which I refer to as the Fayette plates.

Brother Bushman's footnote 63 details the rationale behind this sequence:

> The order of translation has been established through analysis of the handwriting of the original manuscript. The bulk of the writing in the fragments of 1 Nephi that have been saved is in the hand of Oliver Cowdery, with a number of passages in a hand that most resembles John Whitmer's. Anything in these two hands

---

[119] Richard Lyman Bushman, *Joseph Smith: Rough Stone Rolling*, Alfred A. Knopf (New York 2005), p. 74.

must have been written after April 6, when Oliver arrived in Harmony. Oliver's is the first hand to appear, writing 1 Nephi 2:2-23. There is no evidence of Emma Smith's hand, as would be expected had Joseph begun with 1 Nephi after the loss of the first 116 pages. Joseph did not meet John Whitmer until after June 1, 1829, when Joseph and Oliver moved to Fayette from Harmony. Thus it is unlikely that Emma and Joseph began work on 1 Nephi in the winter of 1829 when they resumed translating. Work on 1 Nephi probably began in late May. It also appears that the Book of Mosiah in the current Book of Mormon is not complete. It begins abruptly without the introduction that Mormon affixed to all the other books he abridged. Possibly the first pages of Mosiah were among the 116 that were lost. The evidence implies Joseph and Oliver began work on Mosiah when they began translating together in April 1829, finished the book to the end, and then went back and translated 1 Nephi up through Mosiah. The handwriting analysis was accomplished by Dean Jessee and presented in "Mormon Manuscript," 259-78."

Appendix 7: Accounts of the Trip to Fayette

David Whitmer is the main source for the important trip to Fayette, but Lucy Mack Smith also discussed it. I have put the accounts from both of them online at https://www.lettervii.com/p/trip-to-fayette-references.html and www.mobom.org.

Appendix 8: Philosophical Implications

Philosophical implications don't usually belong in a history book, but the implications of the 116 pages and the small plates of Nephi that replaced them have been widely discussed, so I'm making a comment here.

The traditional faithful narrative holds that around 380 A.D., when Mormon was abridging the records of the Nephites, the Lord knew that in 1828 A.D., Martin Harris was going to act as scribe for Joseph Smith, that when they had written 116 pages of manuscript Harris was going to desire to show the manuscript to his wife and a few others, that someone was going to steal the manuscript, and that it would never be found (as of this writing).

With this foreknowledge, the Lord inspired Mormon to add the small plates of Nephi to his abridgment to "replace" the content of the 116 pages, the premise being that the small plates covered roughly the same material as the Book of Lehi.

I think this is a misreading of Words of Mormon, as I explain in this book.

The traditional interpretation is often used to explain the foreknowledge of God. For some, this is a troubling concept.

Whatever Happened to the Golden Plates?

Joseph received two revelations about the lost 116 pages (D&C 3 and 10) that describe Harris as "a wicked man." Was he wicked because of the choice he made in 1828, or was he wicked hundreds of years before he was born and he just played out his predetermined role?

And if that was the case for Harris, is it the case for us?

Philosophers have debated this question without resolution. The most common explanation seems to be that God knows us so well he knows exactly what we'll do—he knows in advance every single decision and thought we'll have throughout our lives.

But what if the small plates of Nephi were *not* in the stone box, as I propose? If they, along with piles of other Nephite records, were available in the nearby repository in the Hill Cumorah, then the Lord was prepared for any contingency as Joseph and his scribes embarked on the high-stakes endeavor to translate and publish the ancient record. Martin Harris was not predestined to sin.

This is a simplified analysis, but for me, it's a nice resolution of the philosophical issue.

Appendix 9: Two-Cumorahs background

For many years, there has been a scholarly theory that rejects what Joseph and Oliver taught about the Hill Cumorah in New York. Instead, proponents teach a "two-Cumorahs" theory to support the idea that the Book of Mormon took place in Central America (primarily in Mesoamerica, meaning southern Mexico and Guatemala—the home of the Mayans).

They rationalize that New York is too far away from Mesoamerica to be the scene of the final battles of the Nephites and Jaredites. Therefore, they say, Joseph and Oliver were merely ignorant speculators when they said these final battles took place in New York.

Proponents of the two-Cumorahs theory say Joseph and Oliver misled the Church in Letter VII and D&C 128 and that their successors—including prophets and apostles who have spoken about the New York Cumorah in General Conference—have perpetuated a false tradition.

Maybe you aren't aware of the two-Cumorahs theory, but you've definitely learned it if you've been taught the Mesoamerican setting for the Book of Mormon.

In a sense, why should we care that LDS scholars and educators teach the two-Cumorahs theory? They're entitled to academic freedom and they can say whatever they want. They are good people, faithful members of the Church who want to build faith and not destroy it.

But in this case, their teachings have created two problems.

1. This two-Cumorahs theory undermines faith.

Joseph Fielding Smith was Church Historian and had been a member of the Quorum of the Twelve Apostles for twenty years when he became alarmed at the development of the two-Cumorahs theory in the 1920s and 1930s.

The theory originated with scholars from the Reorganized Church of Jesus Christ of Latter-day Saints. They taught that Cumorah could not be in New York because the text describes a limited geography, and it had to be somewhere in Central America.

Consequently, the hill in New York is merely the place where Moroni deposited the plates. It's "Moroni's Hill." It was incorrectly named Cumorah by early saints who didn't know better, and Joseph adopted this false tradition.

The theory claims that the "real" Hill Cumorah, the scene of the final battles and the repository of the records (Mormon 6:6), is "Mormon's Hill" and it is somewhere in southern Mexico.

In response, President Smith reiterated that Cumorah is in New York. Referring to the two-Cumorahs theory, he wrote: *"Because of this theory some members of the Church have become confused and greatly disturbed in their faith in the Book of Mormon."*

LDS scholars ignored his warning and eventually the two-Cumorahs theory was widely adopted.

President Smith repeated the same warning when he was President of the Quorum of the Twelve in the 1950s, but again the scholars rejected his counsel.

You don't have to look very far today to see that "some members of the Church have become confused and greatly disturbed in their faith in the Book of Mormon."

And the impact on investigators is just as devastating.

Put yourself in the position of an investigator—or a youth in the Church—and imagine how confusing it is to be told by the missionaries or your Seminary teacher that Joseph and Oliver told the truth about everything *except* what they taught about Cumorah in New York. On that point, you're supposed to believe because of the two-Cumorahs theory, they were ignorant speculators who misled the Church.

President Smith's warning is almost an understatement of the devastating impact the two-Cumorahs theory is having in the Church today.

But as I said, why should we care what LDS scholars say? Every prophet and apostle who has spoken about Cumorah has reiterated the New York location, including in General Conference.

Here's the second problem:

2. This two-Cumorahs theory has prevailed in the Church.

You might be thinking, "I have never heard of a two-Cumorahs theory. What is he talking about?"

It's a good question.

In my experience, many active members of the Church believe Cumorah is in New York. They don't realize how pervasive the two-Cumorahs theory has become.

Every time you see an illustration of the Book of Mormon that includes a Mayan jungle or pyramid, you are seeing a presentation of the two-Cumorahs theory.

If you have a missionary or foreign-language edition of the Book of Mormon published in 1981 or later (the blue book), open it to the illustrations at the beginning. They teach the two-Cumorahs theory.

You see it on display in the North Visitors Center on Temple Square in Salt Lake City. First, there is "Mormon's Cumorah;" i.e., the exhibit showing Mormon abridging the Nephite records in a cave full of records (Mormon 6:6) that is decorated with Mayan glyphs (depicting Mesoamerica).

Across the hall, in a separate display, is "Moroni's Cumorah" where Moroni is burying the plates in the New York.

How and why has the two-Cumorahs theory prevailed?

The complete answer is beyond the scope of this book (I've addressed it in several other books), but I think the most basic answer is this: members of the Church have never heard of Letter VII.

In Joseph Smith's day, everyone knew about Letter VII. He had it copied into his personal history. Letter VII was reprinted in all Church magazines, starting with the 1835 *Messenger and Advocate*, and continuing through the *Improvement Era*, so everyone could read it. As a result, for the first hundred years of this dispensation, everyone knew Cumorah—the real Cumorah—was in New York.

But Letter VII has never been published in the *Ensign*.

It is not in the modern lesson manuals.

Because the Mesoamerican theory depends on the two-Cumorahs theory, proponents have managed to keep Letter VII out of their scholarly publications. They don't cite it. They don't address it. They don't even want people to know about it.

To reiterate, I'm not questioning the motives of these scholars and educators. They're good people, faithful members of the Church who want to build faith, not destroy it. I wrote the book *Mesomania* to examine the psychology that underlies the two-Cumorahs theory.

Motives have nothing to do with this.

Joseph Fielding Smith didn't care about motives. He cared about the devastating impact on faith that the two-Cumorahs theory causes.

If you'd like to know more about this, read Chapter 2 of my *Letter VII* book.

There has never been a better time for studying Church history than the present. The more we learn, the more we appreciate the prophetic calling and ministry of Joseph Smith and his associates and successors.

The New York Cumorah doesn't answer all the questions about Book of Mormon geography, but it does enhance our understanding of early Church history and, I believe, helps sustain our faith and confidence in the early Brethren who participated in the restoration of the Gospel of Jesus Christ in these latter days.

Figure 5 - Reenactment of translation table

Re-enactment of the table where Joseph Smith and Oliver Cowdery translated the Book of Mormon in Joseph's rebuilt home at the Priesthood Restoration Site in Oakland Township, Pennsylvania (formerly Harmony, PA). Photo by author.

Made in the USA
Coppell, TX
21 January 2026